FASCINATION WITH FIBER

Fascination with Fiber

MICHIGAN'S HANDWEAVING HERITAGE

Marie A. Gile and Marion T. Marzolf

In Partnership with the
MICHIGAN STATE UNIVERSITY MUSEUM

THE UNIVERSITY OF MICHIGAN PRESS
Ann Arbor

2009   2008   2007   2006   4   3   2   1

A CIP catalog record for this book is available from the British Library.

Library of Congress Cataloging-in-Publication Data

Gile, Marie A.
   Fascination with fiber : Michigan's handweaving heritage /
Marie A. Gile and Marion T. Marzolf ; in partnership with the
Michigan State University Museum.
       p.   cm.
   Includes bibliographical references.
   ISBN-13: 978-0-472-03113-9 (paper : alk. paper)
   ISBN-10: 0-472-03113-9 (paper : alk. paper)
   1. Hand weaving—Michigan.   2. Textile fabrics—
Michigan.   3. Fiberwork—Michigan.   I. Marzolf, Marion T.
II. Michigan State University Museum.   III. Title.

NK8912.G55   2006
746.1′409774—dc22   2005031393

Text design by Mary H. Sexton
Typesetting by Agnew's, Grand Rapids, Michigan

The text face is FFQuadraat, designed by Fred Smeijers,
launched by FontShop International in 1992.
—Courtesy fontfont.com

The display font is Triplex Serif, designed in 1989 by
Zuzana Licko, co-founder of Émigré.
—Courtesy emigre.com

Foreword

That fascination with fiber runs deep in Michigan is evident in the narrative that follows. In it, Marie Gile and Marion Marzolf, the authors of this comprehensive history of weaving in the Great Lakes State, chronicle the evolution of textile production from the late eighteenth century to the present. What emerges is an account of the vitality and enduring nature of textiles and their transformation from a culture of need and survival to today's aesthetic enjoyment of art fabric.

Like the rest of the country, Michigan attracted immigrants who enriched its way of life. They hailed from countries where handicrafts and weaving were traditionally strong. Despite initial hardships and lack of equipment, the practice of making useful and beautiful fabrics for the household continued in the new country, initially on crude handmade looms. From linens to coverlets to rugs, ethnic European textiles took on the spirit of the New World, resulting in a distinctly American expression. Improvement in lifestyle and easier access to commercial cloth did not, however, diminish the desire to weave. Not even the onset of the Industrial Revolution and the proliferation of textile mills would doom handweaving entirely. To the contrary, the pleasure of the process and the ability to fashion unique items continued and created opportunities for interaction, for learning from others and sharing in the pride of accomplishment. This led, at the beginning of the twentieth century, to a revival of the handicrafts and a renewed interest in keeping traditions alive.

Weaving, however, was more than a private pastime, more than nostalgia or the welcome augmentation of the family budget; it emerged as an integral part of Michigan's economic fabric of life. Since it requires not only physical dexterity but intellectual and aesthetic judgment, it became the perfect medium for art therapy. Hospitals initiated programs that served physically impaired veterans of both world wars as well as mental patients. In turn, the need for suitable instructors led colleges and universities to add weaving courses to their domestic science, home economics, and art curricula.

There was no dearth of artistic initiative. This book's chapter on Hartland vividly describes the formation of an ideal community of like-minded people drawn together by their love of textiles. In a similar but more professional vein, the establishment of Cranbrook Academy of Art in the mid-twenties made Michigan the destination for serious students from all over the country and the world. Initially representing the modernist Scandinavian aesthetic, it developed into one of America's preeminent art academies. Some of the best-known fiber artists and teachers as well as recognized leaders in the textile industry are Cranbrook graduates. Hartland and Cranbrook, each in its own way, fostered a strong community spirit, which inspired weavers to come together in many parts of the state.

The formation of weavers' guilds, which Michigan experienced during and after World War II, was a direct result of this resurgence in the craft. Such leaders as Mary Meigs Atwater, Mary Black, and Harriet Tidball provided guidance, encouragement, and practical advice through newsletters and meetings. Craft fairs, museums, and yarn shops proliferated and supported the burgeoning guild movement, which, in 1959, culminated in the formation of the Michigan League of Handweavers. This organization, still flourishing today, promotes study groups, lectures, and traveling exhibitions enabling individual guilds throughout the state to share these events as well as the expertise of visiting instructors, many from abroad. The Michigan League of Handweavers History Project Collection at the Michigan State University Museum in East Lansing is a fitting memorial to the efforts of pioneering visionaries.

In Michigan, textiles have played different roles at different times. They indisputably impacted the state's economic, academic, and artistic life. Beyond that, they fostered bonds among like-minded people and cemented lifelong friendships formed through a determined devotion to reach across the state. Documenting the rich historic legacy of textiles in Michigan is a remarkable achievement of this book's authors.

Sigrid Wortmann Weltge

Preface

Fascination with Fiber: Michigan's Handweaving Heritage began as many exhibition and publication projects do, with someone with real passion and intellectual curiosity. What followed has been a remarkable journey that has led to the first truly comprehensive examination of handweaving in Michigan. Many have joined in this research, and the result has provided scholars and the public a deeper appreciation of the people, community organizations, businesses, and institutions that have shaped the vitality of handweaving in Michigan.

Museums are more than stewards of collections. They are, at their best, both places to incubate new ideas and also centers of community engagement, places where a scholar can find like-minded colleagues and where those with shared interests can meet and take action. The staff of the Michigan State University Museum was pleased to embrace this publication project and to watch those involved become immersed in the experience of handweaving in Michigan. We especially valued the opportunity to work with the Michigan League of Handweavers and the many guilds and weavers who joined this collaborative project.

The story of *Fascination with Fiber* began with the passion of Marie Gile, who shared with others her vision to tell the story of handweaving in Michigan. What she brought to this effort, however, extended well beyond a single-minded passion for weaving to a deeply felt respect for all who weave, and a contagious nature for weaving that enabled her to energize others. The result has been true groundbreaking scholarship that brings together the grassroots history of weaving on the community level, the influence of popular culture on weaving practices, the emergence of the guilds' initial formal organizations to support and educate weavers, and the creation of the first college- and university-based formal educational programs for handweaving. Beyond these developments, this project also tells the story of the master weavers, loom builders, woolen mills, and organizational leaders who have contributed to our understanding of handweaving as a dynamic form of artistic expression.

Fascination with Fiber, the exhibit and the book, provide a new perspective on the state of Michigan. Weaving can be understood as being shaped on the community level by oral tradition and initiation, as many weavers learned within the family or community context both how to weave and what to weave. Weaving can also be appreciated as a social activity where weavers gathered to learn from one another to improve skills and share stories. In addition, weaving can be viewed as a way to examine cultural knowledge systems, as immigrants from England, Germany, the Netherlands, Sweden, and Finland brought their traditions with them and sustained those traditions. Finally, this project demonstrates that weaving today has overcome the status as a "lesser" art form to take its place in the canon of art and design.

The Michigan State University Museum has been especially pleased to participate in the *Fascination with Fiber* exhibition project. The museum has a commitment to the documentation, preservation, and presentation of the artistic and cultural traditions of Michigan. Working in partnership with the Michigan Council for the Arts and Cultural Affairs and the Michigan Department of History, Arts, and Libraries, the museum has sought to focus on cultural forms and forms of traditional arts, folk arts, and rural arts that are often overlooked or not fully understood as part of Michigan's creative and artistic legacy. Our Michigan Traditional Arts Program and Rural Arts and Culture Program, administrated in conjunction with the Michigan Council for the Arts and Cultural Affairs, have helped contribute to such projects as *Fascination with Fiber*. In addition, the *Fascination with Fiber* exhibition will be circulated to other museums by the Michigan State University Traveling Exhibition Service. We are grateful to the funding agencies, organizations, and individuals who contributed the financial resources for this multifaceted project.

In the years to come, much more will be learned about the rich history of handweaving in Michigan. The Michigan State University Museum has continued to build a central archive for oral histories and documentation on handweaving in Michigan, for scholars, weavers, and the general public. We are both honored and pleased to host and share these museum resources for generations to come.

Fascination with Fiber has been a truly inspirational journey. The voices of weavers, past and present, enrich our lives. We at the Michigan State University Museum are deeply grateful to Marie Gile and Marion Marzolf for this extraordinary book, which will take its place as an essential resource for all who study Michigan's artistic and cultural history. We very much appreciate the University of Michigan Press for having early interest and unwavering belief in this book and for partnering with the Michigan State University Museum to share this rich story of weavers and weaving in Michigan.

C. Kurt Dewhurst, PhD
Director, Michigan State University Museum

Acknowledgments

This book began on the wave of energy generated by an exhibition about subjects close to our hearts—handweaving, fiber arts, and history. We would like to thank the many organizations and individuals who have so generously shared their thoughts, time, and energy and have inspired us in this work.

We are deeply grateful to our editor, Mary Erwin, for her constant help and sage advice, and to C. Kurt Dewhurst, director of the Michigan State University Museum, for his continued support and encouragement.

Thank you to Sigrid Weltge for her very helpful comments about our early draft, to Bernice Sizemore for especially helpful information, to Martha Brownscombe for her insightful comments on the chapters about the guilds and trends of the times, to Dolores Slowinski for Detroit insights, to JoAnn Bachelder for much-needed help filling in some of our omissions, and especially to Reade Dornan for her constructive and candid reading of the draft, which helped us focus our work.

Thank you to all the guilds and individuals in the Michigan League of Handweavers (MLH) for your support and help in documenting guild histories, to the MLH Board for its encouragement, and especially to MLH members Peggy Adams, JoAnn Bachelder, Patty Beyer, Martha Brownscombe, Pat Chipman, Nadine Cloutier, Millie Danielson, Helen Griffiths, Lestra Hazel, Leslie Johnson, Kris Krumanaker, Midge Lewis, Dianne Little, Loretta Oliver, Nancy Peck, Mary Lou Reichard, Pat Rowley, Bernice Sizemore, Rita Swartz, Diane VanderPol, Barbara VanDyke, Sue Walton, and Margaret Windeknecht for their volunteer work on the project.

We appreciate the expert work by the Michigan State University Museum and staff, who helped make the exhibition possible and were supportive in innumerable ways. In particular, we thank Juan Alvarez, Michele Beltran, Judy DeJaegher, Beth Donaldson, Francie Freese, Lori Helou, Latricia Horstman, Julie Levy-Weston, Yvonne Lockwood, Marsha MacDowell, Bill Matt, Tammy Stone-Gordon, Pearl Yee Wong, Mary Worrall, and especially director Kurt Dewhurst, coordinator Julie Avery, project director Lynne

Swanson, and exhibit designer Melinda Hamilton. For their significant contributions to the exhibit, we thank East Lansing Masonic Lodge 480, Free and Accepted Masons; the MEEMIC Foundation for the Future of Education; the Michigan Council for Arts and Cultural Affairs; the Michigan Humanities Council; the Michigan League of Handweavers; and the National Endowment for the Humanities.

Historical research was facilitated by the helpful staffs at Cranbrook Archives of Cranbrook Academy of Art, the Central Michigan University Libraries, the Cromaine District Library, the Eastern Michigan University Bruce T. Halle Library and Archives, the Hartland Area Historical Society, the State Archives of Michigan, the Michigan State University Museum Archives, Benson Ford Research Center at The Henry Ford, Wayne State University's Walter P. Reuther Library, and the Western Michigan University Libraries. So very helpful in providing artist information, photos, textiles, and artifacts were William Colburn, Mary Jane Drilling, Faye Sketchley, and members of the Libby Crawford family.

To everyone who, over many years, shared their memories and thoughts on tape, by phone, or e-mail, with us personally or with other interviewers, thank you for your stories and comments, which made this such a rewarding journey. If we have not personally thanked each one of you who has helped us along the way, we thank you now. We especially thank our husbands, Harvey Gile and Kingsbury Marzolf, for their patience and help as we have traveled this road together.

Marie A. Gile and Marion T. Marzolf

Contents

Introduction

What Keeps Craft Alive?

What keeps the craft of handweaving alive? What is so special about this craft or any craft? Why does it thrive, and what will keep it alive for the future? At work are huge forces that have been important in the past, it seems, and that remain important today. It is not one institution or idea. In Michigan, craft is kept alive by a very complex network. Guilds have brought individuals together to learn, share, and encourage members. There has been intense interest in bringing to the state leaders from around the United States, as well as excellent local Michigan teachers, to present workshops and programs for guilds and conferences. Statewide art associations and shops—where weaving is taught on a regular basis and where prominent individuals come to teach—have been a boon to guilds and individuals, supporting local guilds and the Michigan League of Handweavers in various ways. Museums and various groups have sponsored fiber exhibits. University teachers have offered in-depth and challenging courses. National movements have resulted in such organizations as the Handweavers Guild of America. Each one of these factors is a part of the interwoven network that keeps handweaving and fiber arts fascinating, active, and alive.

Michigan's weaving and fiber arts have a long history that began with the early settlers (Dutch, English, Finns, French Canadians, Germans, Irish, Michigan American Indians, Scots, and Swedes) and continued through Michigan's statehood. This history included many ethnic weaving traditions. The Arts and Crafts and the Bauhaus movements of the early twentieth century and the founding of Cranbrook Academy of Art in the 1920s shaped it. In the 1930s, Hartland, Michigan, developed into a significant national weaving region. Products from Cromaine Crafts in Hartland were sold from New York to Chicago. Hartland attracted national attention by inviting Mary Atwater, the "dean of American handweaving," to Michigan to lead the first of many national weaving conferences. Michigan supplied major weavers to the United States and was at the forefront in the resurgence of handweaving in the 1950s and 1960s. During the 1970s, Michigan was a vital part of the national fiber movement that generated new interests in all the crafts, but particularly handweaving. Michigan became the place where the national Handweavers Guild of America held its first conference in 1972. The 1980s and 1990s saw the flowering of interest in computer technology and surface design in weaving and the expansion into all areas of fiber arts.

The story of handweaving and fiber arts in Michigan is also the story of the histories of its weaving guilds and weaving institutions. It is the values, ideas, and thoughts related to these histories as revealed through the words and works of its weavers and guilds. Oral histories help interpret experiences of the past and the role of weavers and guilds within the community. By recording and sharing their memories, visions, and dreams, weavers have documented their own and their guilds' histories and linked them with those of the statewide network—the Michigan League of Handweavers—and the national Handweavers Guild of America. Guild researchers have uncovered stories of past guild and community activities that work toward reenergizing and revitalizing their guild and its relationships with the community.

Today, the Internet adds depth to this network, offering fiber artists and guild members a link to connect immediately with other artists and members, to access information about textile events and people worldwide, to seek and offer textile knowledge, and to inform the public of guild and textile activities. Undoubtedly, new ideas and innovations will further enrich our abilities to network and connect with other fiber artists and craftspeople.

ONE

The Early Years

For centuries, textiles have been produced to keep humans warm and protected and to furnish their homes. Need drives the work, whether by hand or in the factory, but even in the most primitive circumstances, purely functional and elaborate artistic pieces exist side by side. In the United States, the hand loom was common in colonial and frontier pioneer homesteads. Small mills for wool preparation dotted the waterways in the Midwest as settlements moved south and westward.

Prior to the Industrial Revolution (about 1770–1850), when textile production "shifted from rural handicraft to urban factories," all textiles were handwoven.[1] The British protective Wool Act of 1699 banned shipping of American-made wool—raw materials and textiles.[2] However, American textile mills of New England grew and later became a force in world trade. The cheaply produced cotton fabrics and the fine-quality woolens available from the factories quickly threatened the survival of hand production. Factory goods were readily available throughout the land in the nineteenth century due to the cheaper transportation of raw materials and finished goods on the Erie Canal and the railroads. The Civil War kept some small mills in the Midwest and South in business, but the postwar industrial growth and, later, the 1930s depression spelled the end for most of them.

Despite nearly becoming a lost art and craft, weaving enjoyed a revival, with other crafts, in the early twentieth century. Across the United States, handweaving as an art form or design tool, a profitable hobby, and a recreational or therapeutic activity kept the hand loom and spinning wheel in motion. The New England factories that had grown to massive size with labor-saving innovations moved to the South and abroad to save on labor costs, leaving behind empty buildings. These have become the weavers' historical legacy as textile museums or other rehabilitated structures. Through all this, weaving continued, revived by individuals, communities, art schools, hospitals, and social agencies. These, in turn, inspired the formation and growth of arts and crafts guilds, national meetings, and arts and crafts publications that maintain the viability of weaving as a craft and a fine art.

The Michigan handweaving story is mostly a twentieth-century one. However, the home weaver and the itinerant weaver were practicing their craft in 1837, when the agricultural state of Michigan was granted statehood. They still could be found in small Michigan communities in 1900, when the state's population had grown to 1.6 million, with 68.2 percent living in urban areas.[3] Artists and skilled craftspeople had been attracted to Michigan's early furniture center in Grand Rapids and Zeeland, Michigan, and to the auto industry in Detroit. Their work contributed to these new products, as well as to the decoration of public buildings and homes and to the growth of technical and arts and crafts schools and colleges.

Immigrants from Sweden, Finland, England, Germany, and the Netherlands brought with them the knowledge of weaving and spinning. Michigan's museums contain textiles, hand looms, and spinning wheels that reflect this heritage, even though written documentation is sometimes scant. Memories of these family crafts are alive today. If you set up a loom in a public location, you will be approached by a surprising number of senior citizens who exclaim: "Why, my mother [or grandmother, aunt, or neighbor] used to do this. I thought it was a dying art."[4]

The reports of life in Michigan's pioneer settlements relate stories of life in the woods and how the land was cleared for early farms. Michigan was settled later than might be expected, because first reports about the state emphasized extensive swampland and fever epidemics. But in the 1830s and 1840s, villages and farms were growing along the state's southern border, from Lake Michigan to the Detroit area. These locations were mostly settled by New Englanders making a move for better lives and available land.

In the village of Pontiac, north of Detroit, in 1838, Mary Lewis (b. 1811), a native of Windsor, Vermont, married and began housekeeping. Her daughter recalled that she was "one of those thrifty New England women," who made her own table and other linen to furnish her new log house. Mary's daughter wrote: "I have often heard the neighbors tell how she could spin her two days work in one, in the long summer days. I often counted the knots to see how fast she was getting along." Each knot marked sixty yards of spun wool.[5] The family raised fields of flax, and Mary carded, spun, and wove it. Her daughter helped with the spinning and hatcheling (combing) of the flax. In her early years of married life, Mary Lewis also helped with farmwork and spun for others. Mary's neighbors recalled that "her family was supplied with all the necessary woolen garments for winter, from the woolen socks and stockings, to the dresses, coats, and pants, besides all the wool home-made blankets and sheets for the beds." Mary's hand-built loom was in use for over twenty years. Her weaving added up to fourteen hundred yards a year and helped pay for necessities.[6]

Not every Michigan pioneer family home contained a loom, of course, but most pioneer women could spin, knit, and sew. As times improved, one pioneer recalled: "Mother spun, wove, colored, and made up the wearing apparel for her whole family, until the invention of machinery and the incoming railroad changed everything and made home manufactures unprofitable. Suddenly all the female world found itself genteel in calico at twelve and a half cents and delaine [plain-weave wool] at twenty-five cents per yard, then the spinning wheel and loom were put aside."[7]

Many of the early looms in colonial America and pioneer Michigan homes were sturdy "barn looms" made of hand-hewn, seasoned-wood uprights. Their beams and frames were fastened with wooden pegs. A loom with two harnesses (shafts) could be used for rugs and blankets and plain-weave cloth, while one with four allowed twills and fancy weaves. Typically, these looms were forty to sixty inches square and around six feet high.[8] They could take up nearly as much space as a four-poster bed and sometimes were kept in outbuildings or attics when not in use. Looms were bulky to transport across the ocean, but spinning wheels could easily fit in an immigrant's trunk. Father Gabriel Richard, a Catholic priest in Detroit during 1801–11, brought three dozen wheels and one loom for his primary school. He taught young native women to raise hemp, flax, and sheep and to spin and weave their own cloth.[9] Both the smaller Colonial or Saxony wheels for spinning flax or wool and the large walking wheels for wool were utilized by settlers in early Michigan. Most of this equipment was brought into Michigan from elsewhere until the late 1800s, when a few Germanic-style flyer wheels were being produced in Monroe and Traverse City by unnamed wheelmakers.[10]

At the time Father Richard taught Native American women the uses of hemp, flax, and wool in the early 1800s, the tribes in Michigan were creating a variety of items that were woven. The Ottawa (Odawa), Potawatomi, and Chippewa (Ojibwa) wove mats, storage bags, and medicine pouches from natural and animal fibers. The fibers used for these domestic and religious/sacred textiles were often nettle (a bast fiber) and buffalo hair; rushes and cattails were used in weaving mats. The products were decorated with geometric patterns, thunderbirds, underwater panthers, and other motifs.

After contact with European cultures and the introduction of commercial wool yarns and beads, clothing that had been made from animal hides could begin to include these new materials. Also being adopted were methods of European weaving and needlework. Various styles of finger-weaving were done, the most common being plaiting and twining. The traditional sash with long fringes was now fingerwoven with fine wool yarns and embellished with trade beads, which replaced the fringes of wrapped porcupine quills made in the past. The sash was usually worn as a decorative item, often wrapped around the waist, sometimes over the shoulder, or sometimes as a turban by the men. For traveling purposes, sacred objects in the medicine bundle could be wrapped in a sash or in a finely woven mat. A woven garter, adorning both men and women, was worn just below the knee to fasten buckskin leggings. A new clothing style, the bandolier bag, was adopted by the Chippewa (Ojibwa) after European contact. The women added handwoven shoulder straps (bandoliers) to their traditional bags and pouches (also adding trade materials, ribbon, glass, and metallic beads), making the bag not only functional for wearing but decorative as well.[11]

The Professional Coverlet Weavers

Skilled Irish, English, and German immigrant weavers, whose livelihood was endangered by the growing textile industry, came to America. Most often they and their families farmed and wove in their new homes. One of their products was the fancy-weave coverlet. Such coverlets were valued by nineteenth-century middle-class farm and business families as gifts for weddings, births, anniversaries, and other special occasions. They were warm and decorative and made handsome and useful bedcovers, with indigo blue or madder red designs against a natural cotton field. Although a decorative coverlet in overshot, summer and winter, or double weave could be woven on the hand loom, most of the coverlets that survived as family heirlooms in New England and the Midwest were made by professional weavers using a Jacquard attachment to their looms. By the end of the Civil War, the coverlet was out of fashion, so weavers made carpets or other useful household linens.[12]

The Jacquard attachment, which was added to the loom, was invented by Joseph Marie Jacquard in France in 1803 and introduced in America in 1826. A strong floor loom with a Jacquard attachment took up six square feet of space and needed twelve feet in height to accommodate the long sheaf of several hundred punched cards that selected the proper threads for each row of the design. A design might be repeated every twelve to seventeen inches. Similar to the piano roll or early computer punch cards, the French invention revolutionized weaving, making it possible to lift individual threads in many combinations in order to make elaborate designs, often floral.[13] The weaver would generally set up shop in an area, announce the business in the local newspaper, then ride out to meet prospective clients. Work was done in the shop. Michigan has three documented Jacquard coverlet weavers—Philip Allabach, Enos Michael, and Abram William Van Doren—whose works are in museum and private collections. Their coverlets were woven in double weave and tied Beiderwand (a traditional German weave). Van Doren was the only one who worked solely in Michigan, and researcher Katharine Brown located twenty-eight of his

FASCINATION WITH FIBER

coverlets for her master's thesis. Eleven are in museums, including the Michigan State University Museum, the Detroit Institute of Arts, and the Art Institute of Chicago.[14]

Van Doren (1808–84) came from a Dutch family of fourteen children settled in New Jersey. Four of the brothers in the family were weavers. Abram apparently learned the craft at home, then married and moved to Michigan in 1844 to set up his own shop with equipment he purchased in the East. He settled in Rochester, Avon Township, in Oakland County, near the mills on Stony Creek, where he maintained his business until 1851. He advertised and wove his name, the location, the date, and the client's name into the corner block of his coverlets. Brown noted that all of his coverlets she examined used the Double Rose or Double Lily pattern associated with his family and were made for customers who lived within ten miles of his shop.[15] The weaver provided the natural cotton warp, and the customer brought in handspun wool for the pattern threads. Van Doren's coverlets varied in size to fit three-quarter, full, and small beds, but several were around seventy-three by eighty inches. Based on the 1851 account book of Benjamin Crissman, owner of the Buckhorn Tavern in Romeo, Van Doren charged $9.50 for the weaving of three coverlets. He entered a coverlet in the first Michigan State Fair in 1849, winning first place. He won awards three years in a row.[16] By 1860, Van Doren had moved to Ionia County, where he was listed as a weaver and later a farmer. He died in 1884, en route to California with his wife to join their son.[17]

Michigan Wool and Mill Towns

Sheep and wool production were important in Michigan until the early twentieth century. In the 1860s, Washtenaw, Oakland, Jackson, Calhoun, Lenawee, and Livingston counties in southern Michigan raised 40 percent of the state's wool output. Between 1860 and 1910, Michigan was the highest producer of sheep among eleven midwestern states, with a peak number of 4,029,000 sheep in 1867, falling to 1,505,000 in 1910.[18] Several factors account for the decline. The Civil War had increased demand for textiles, because imports were difficult to obtain, so local production went up temporarily but declined when imports resumed. The demand for fine-quality merino wool for clothing increased, but the large merino herds and grazing lands were located in the West.[19]

After World War I, imported wools dominated the market. Prices dropped, and large mills grew larger, so many small mills closed. Typically, the small midwestern woolen mill produced coarse fabric for blankets, outdoor sportswear, and work clothes. Much of the state's wool clip was sold to the New England mills. In 1976, Michigan still produced 1,150,000 pounds of wool, but Texas produced over 20,000,000 pounds, or one-fifth the

Wool coverlet made by Abram Van Doren on a Jacquard loom in the Rochester Hills area of Oakland County, 1844. (Photo by Pearl Yee Wong. Courtesy of the Michigan State University Museum.)

national total.[20] In the late twentieth century, sheep flocks became a side-line crop for Michigan farmers or a retirement hobby.

There were at least thirty-four woolen mills in the state, including those in Alpena, Hastings, Eaton Rapids, Sault Sainte Marie, Morenci, Vassar, Clinton, and Frankenmuth. Some small Michigan mills survived into the twentieth century by developing new specialties, such as ready-made clothing, carriage and automobile cloth, and baseball cores. The knitting

⊹   FASCINATION WITH FIBER

mills in Grand Rapids and Muskegon, for example, produced many lines of clothing. Some mills prepared the yarn only, while others produced fabric and garments. The silk mills at Belding made sewing thread and silk cloth. A post–Civil War tradition of public shearing of sheep and festivals, held to increase community interest in these activities, was revived in the late twentieth century and continues today in several Michigan communities, with sheep-to-shawl competitions.[21] Observers enjoy the excitement of seeing the shearing of sheep, the making of wool yarn, and the weaving of a wool shawl in one day by experts in these crafts. Handweaving and spinning remain categories in the Michigan State Fair competitions.

In 1925, Ford Motor Company opened its own experimental woolen mill at the Highland Park Plant, to manufacture wool for automobile interiors. The plant could produce thirty-five hundred to four thousand yards per day, but the auto factory used twenty-two thousand yards daily.[22] Starting in 1926, Ford buyers personally inspected local sheep in southern Michigan and purchased wool pelts. They needed a midlevel type of wool—neither too coarse nor too fine—which came from Shropshire, Hampshire, or Southdown sheep. Experts in animal husbandry from Michigan State College consulted with Ford on ways to improve the Michigan breeds.[23] But in 1930, Ford closed its plant and relied on outside sources for its fabrics. The Highland Park Plant was then used to develop experimental parts and supplies, including synthetic leather and rubber. The Yale Woolen Mill

Scene from a Michigan mill's postcard with the caption "Making Skeins," ca. 1890s. (Photo courtesy of the State Archives of Michigan.)

Dressing yarn warps at Horner Woolen Mill, 1958–59. (Photo courtesy of the State Archives of Michigan.)

(1881–1963), sixty miles northeast of Detroit, was one of Ford's upholstery fabric suppliers.[24]

Eaton Rapids, located on the Grand River, south of Lansing, was the site of several early mills founded by men who had learned the business in England or in New England. A wool-carding mill was started in 1844. Horner Woolen Mill (1880–1955) specialized in blankets. Big Rock Knitting Mill (1917–27) made socks and sweaters.[25] Davidson's Woolen Mill (1921–69) was the only mill in Michigan spinning its own yarn in 1969, when fire destroyed much of the mill. The section that escaped the fire was rebuilt as Davidson's Old Mill Yarn, which continues as a sales outlet for yarns and supplies. In its prime, Davidson spun the yarn for the Spaulding company (which made major-league baseballs) and produced other specialty knitting and weaving yarns, such as those for Canadian-made hunting jackets and for Chimayo rugs of New Mexico.[26]

The Clinton Woolen Manufacturing Company in Clinton began operations in 1866 and expanded into a four-story factory specializing in quality men's clothing. It, too, suffered fires and rebuilding. By 1917, the mill,

Clinton Woolen Mill, view from south side, 1894. (Photo courtesy of the Historical Society of Clinton, Michigan, Archives.)

with two hundred employees, was doing nearly a million dollars in sales. High-quality cloth for military uniforms was produced here during both world wars and earned the plant an Army-Navy "E" Award for excellence in war production in 1942. Operations ceased in 1957, but the building remained in use and was designated a historic building in 1980.[27]

Today, the Zeilinger Wool Company of Frankenmuth has turned the Zeilinger family's traditional mill into one for custom processing of sheep, Angora goat (mohair), alpaca, llama, dog, rabbit, and silk fibers. Most of their customers want the fibers cleaned and carded for handspinning at home. Zeilinger's also produces a line of wool yarn, quilted mattress pads, and comforters. Before starting on their own, Kathy and Gary Zeilinger worked at the Frankenmuth Woolen Mill (begun in 1894), which Kathy's father owned. That mill, now under different ownership, made lumbermen's socks and mittens in the early twentieth century and added a line of quilts, comforters, and roving. Zeilinger's Wool Company is popular with tourists and schoolchildren because it offers mill tours.[28]

The Belding silk mills along the Flat River were begun in 1863 by four brothers who had learned the trade in Massachusetts. The mills made sewing thread for machine and hand sewing and also silk fabric. Located in a small town in rural Michigan, the mills had a large workforce of around four thousand between 1900 and 1932. Silk imported from Italy, Japan, and China was sorted, graded, twisted, spun, and wound into sewing thread and for warp for weaving on large power looms. Men warped the looms and supervised and tended the equipment and dyeing. Young women (three-fourths of the labor force) were the winders, labelers, spoolers, and weavers.[29] Farm girls eager for paid employment were delighted with a dollar a day for sixty hours of work a week instead of helping for free on the family farm. In Belding, they could room and board for two dollars a week in large, respectable boarding houses with other women, make friends, save money for nice clothes, attend church, and go out on dates. Many sent wages home to help their families or saved money for tuition at business school or teaching colleges.[30] The mills were a significant force in the town for over fifty years, until new owners shut down the mills in 1932. Since then, the mill buildings have been razed or converted to new uses. The Belrochton boarding house, built in 1906 to house a hundred women, became the Belding museum in 1985.

Michigan's early textile mills along the rivers and its productive sheep raising contributed to the state's economic health for decades. The professional textile industries did not promote the work of individual craftspeople or draw on the creative artists or craftspeople for their designs in these early years, yet industry and craft owe their beginnings to the earliest discoveries of ways to weave cloth. On Michigan's farms and in its villages in the twentieth century, the individual weaver continued to make useful and beautiful items for the home, even though all kinds of textiles could easily be purchased. Although it is a story that is largely undocumented, old weaving looms and equipment and the towels and blankets tucked away in Michigan's local history museums bear silent testimony to the endurance of this craft.

TWO

The Revival of Handweaving

The factory production of textiles took away the need for home weaving in the modern, industrialized world. Most looms and wheels were put aside, and families moved on. Yet handweaving continued for several reasons. For some weavers, the reason was the joy of creating at the loom. Immigrants brought craft skills to Michigan, and at least a few continued to weave and spin into their old age. For others, weaving was a way to connect with a by-gone past, when life was simple and wholesome, no matter how hard. It was also encouraging that ordinary people could weave something useful and beautiful with their own hands. Sometimes that item was nice enough to sell to augment the family income; experience in the Appalachian Mountains and at urban settlement houses was already demonstrating that. Not only did the work bring pride and pleasure, but occupational therapists had found that handweaving was useful in rehabilitating sick and injured bodies after World War I. Modern educational leaders introduced shop and home economics (which included textiles, weaving, and sewing) in the lower schools and state colleges, because learning the related skills developed muscle and brain coordination and creative thinking. Handcrafted objects were considered useful and often beautiful, and as the century progressed, craft skills were introduced into the art and design schools in the quest for better-looking factory goods and unique and beautiful art objects. These contrasting ideas about the crafts created an especially rich environment for their revival and growth in Michigan.

Historic Preservation

A market for antique handwoven coverlets developed early in the century, along with a growing interest in the preservation of the nation's early heritage in its important civic and domestic buildings. The demand for newly made handwoven coverlets had declined at the end of the nineteenth century, but there was a new interest among collectors and new weavers. In

1912, one of the best-known American coverlet weavers, William H. Rose, known as Weaver Rose, called a meeting at his Rhode Island workshop. At age seventy-three, he was still turning out coverlets and rugs. He gathered together those interested in traditional handweaving and urged them to collect and preserve the old weaving patterns. They formed the Colonial Weavers Association.[1] The patterns they collected and other colonial weavers' drafts were revived and woven again by a new generation of leisure-time weavers. Museums and libraries preserved these artifacts, and the new weavers discovered them. Historic preservationists, seeking to furnish the old buildings with authentic furniture and textiles, also found them useful. Historic preservation of buildings was in its infancy at the start of the century. Life in colonial and pioneer America recalled a vigorous past, fast being lost by modern Americans. Many old buildings simply fell into ruin, but some were restored, including those at the center of Williamsburg, Virginia (1932). Other buildings, like those transported to Greenfield Village in Dearborn, Michigan (1929), were restored and rebuilt in a new open-air museum environment.

The automobile manufacturer Henry Ford had been buying Thomas Edison items and other historic artifacts and restoring his own family farm, the Wayside Inn, and Botsford Tavern west of Detroit before he announced in 1928 that he would create a historic village at Dearborn, modeled on the Skansen open-air museum in Stockholm, Sweden. In building Greenfield Village, he set out to save and restore Americana for the education of present and future generations. In addition to town and dwelling buildings, he brought to the village examples of early industrial shops and equipment, including old hand looms and modern power looms. The 1850 Plymouth Carding Mill and its machinery for carding wool was restored and rebuilt in Greenfield Village and used for demonstrations. On the village grounds, students attended the Edison Institute schools, which ranged from elementary to junior college level. They learned to weave towels, pillow tops, place mats, and the like for sale to the tourists. Ford believed in learning by doing and promoted the vocational skills. Public classes in weaving and other crafts were also held at the village. After Ford died in 1943, the enthusiasm for the schools declined, and they were closed by 1952. The group of textile buildings at Greenfield Village includes the carding mill and the weaving room (with various types of looms) and Hank's Silk Mill from 1810. Guides give visitors a quick overview of the process of making yarns and cloth in the nineteenth century. The current name for the complex including the village, the museum, and the Edison Institute and Archives is The Henry Ford.[2]

Collectors and preservationists were looking back in order to preserve the past for future generations, but another interest in the early twentieth century was the promotion of the arts and crafts for their many healthful, social, and artistic benefits. These forces and the growth of occupational therapy and domestic science in education and as careers created a fertile environment for the revival of handweaving. Homemakers were encouraged to earn extra money through the sale of weaving products. Occupational therapy, a new and growing field at the start of the twentieth century, found weaving a valuable tool in rehabilitation of veterans from World Wars I and II. Weaving was also widely used in Michigan's mental hospitals, including those in Ypsilanti, Kalamazoo, and Traverse City. This activity helped hand-eye coordination; the repetitive rhythm of weaving was soothing, and the touch and color of the fibers seemed healthful. Weaving classes appeared in Michigan's normal schools at Ypsilanti, Kalamazoo, and Mount Pleasant, where they were considered useful for occupational therapy and vocational and elementary education. Colleges with domestic science or home economics programs, such as Michigan State College (now Michigan State University), gave courses in textiles, including handweaving.[3]

The most successful application of reviving old craft skills and weaving for profit was in Appalachia, where several religious-based schools began programs in the early twentieth century to revive the mountain crafts of spinning, weaving, and woodworking. Today's craft centers at Penland, North Carolina, at Arrowmont in Gatlinburg, Tennessee, and at Berea College in Kentucky stem from these origins.[4] Similar goals were promoted for new immigrants at urban settlement houses—such as Hull House in Chicago and Henry Street Settlement in New York City—and in urban churches and YWCAs. In Michigan in the 1930s and 1940s, community programs taught town and farm women to weave to earn extra income. A program in Hartland was featured in *Women's Day* magazine in 1941.[5] The authors of the article informed readers that they had made "a wide survey of the handicraft movement" and were offering everyone a "grand new recipe for an ailing budget." The recipe read, "Any woman with a pair of hands, gumption in her make-up and industry in her system can become an earning part of the great new movement for making things at home."[6]

Loom companies advertised inexpensive looms and even supplied pre-warped beams to customers who would quickly repay their investments with their rug production. The earliest manufacture of looms in Michigan was at Battle Creek, where Dr. William H. Kynette patented the Eureka hand carpet loom in 1885, to replace his wife's old-fashioned loom, which "took up all the spare room in the house." His loom was especially popular for weaving rag carpets, and he believed it to be a "great blessing" to the poor women who could not leave home to work but could earn money weaving rugs. The loom business was such a success that the doctor stopped his work at the Kellogg Sanitarium and ran the loom manufacture until failing health in 1907 caused him to sell out to the Reed Manufacturing Company of Springfield, Ohio.[7]

Early in the twentieth century, conditions were favorable for the development of an organization that would link together the many women learning to weave as part of their professional or home life. It would take shape under the leadership of Mary Meigs Atwater, who, like many others, came to weaving in a roundabout way, but who turned it into a professional career. Atwater studied art at the School of the Art Institute of Chicago and in Paris. She then married and accompanied her husband, a mining engineer, to various sites. In 1916, in Montana, where she began teaching herself to weave, she also sought to help other wives find useful work for the long days at the lonely mining camps. She was inspired by the work-study program at Berea College in Kentucky, where students wove traditional linens and coverlets to earn their tuition. She wrote to anyone she could find who knew about weaving, took apart an old coverlet to study, and found a loom and a teacher. When her husband died, she used her art and weaving to do occupational therapy in army hospitals. Continuing her correspondence with others about weaving, she began museum research to locate weaving patterns to try. When her son entered college at Cambridge, Atwater moved her family there and devoted her full time to writing and teaching. She began a new business in 1922, the Shuttle-Craft Guild. In September 1924, she began publication of the national monthly *Shuttle-Craft Guild Bulletin*, for guild members.[8] Members were invited to take her weaving class in person or by correspondence. In the first issue of the *Bulletin*, she said, "Handweaving is rapidly growing into a large industry, but it is still almost entirely unorganized."[9]

Atwater set about organizing the handweaving industry.[10] She published weaving instructions and developed a new graph system for weaving drafts, showing precisely where to thread, tie up, and treadle. Her earliest sources for weaving patterns were the colonial drafts in museum collections and Swedish weaving books written in Swedish. Her *Bulletin* promoted a philosophy of the highest standards of work, selling prices that were "sufficient to make good work worth doing," and the sharing of information for the improvement of the field and all weavers.[11] In an early issue of the *Bulletin*, Atwater said she already had two hundred members, but after an employee misused her mailing list, she never again shared the membership numbers. Atwater's influence was extensive and increased with the circulation of her publications *A Book of Designs from the John Landes Drawings in the Pennsylvania Museum, Drafts and Notes* (1925) and *The Shuttle-Craft Book of American Handweaving* (1928), which quickly became the American standard.

Atwater's *Bulletin* reported on weaving activities around the nation. She offered reduced prices on yarns and equipment, as well as helpful hints on techniques, dyeing, and color theory. She pointed out that American handweaving had much in common with Swedish weaving, except for a difference in *sett* (threads per inch).[12] She included in the *Bulletin* only a few traditional Swedish patterns—such as rep weave, Jamtlandsdräll (which she renamed crackle weave), double-weave pickup, and pile rugs—but Atwater frequently referred readers to the Swedish books. She also introduced work from other countries, including Africa, Mexico, Guatemala, and Peru. In 1928, she moved back to Montana, where she continued to teach and publish while her son started a beaver farm. She offered her first weaving institute at Palmer Lake, Colorado, in 1937 and opened her studio to summer student-visitors. In 1938, she was invited to direct the first National Weaving Institute at Hartland, Michigan.[13]

Ruth Cross, from Muskegon, was one of the Michigan weavers who attended the early weaving institutes at Hartland with Atwater. She recalled that Atwater "would fly in from Basin, Montana, her home." Cross said that few people flew in the 1930s, as that was the early stages of commercial aviation. But "Atwater always said that the most dangerous part of the flight was the taxi ride to the airport." Cross added that Atwater worked the hardest and longest and slept the least of anyone she had ever known, typing in her room until two or three in the morning. (Atwater loved mysteries and writing them. One of her mysteries, *Crime in Corn Weather*, is still offered for sale.) There were "two things she always brought with her," Cross explained: "Her gun and her typewriter. She said everyone there [in Montana] always carried a gun and it was safe to go anyplace. We never saw the gun." From their first meeting in 1939 at Waldenwoods in Hartland, Ruth Cross and Mary Atwater became good friends and kept up a correspondence between conferences.[14]

In 1946, Atwater sold the *Bulletin* to Harriet Tidball. She revised her first weaving book in 1951. She published *Byways in Hand-Weaving* in 1954 and started a revision of *Recipe Book* (1933), which was completed and published by the Mary M. Atwater Weavers' Guild in 1957 shortly after Atwater's death. In her later years, she traveled to Guatemala and Mexico, seeking out other modes of handweaving for her writing. She died at age seventy-eight in 1956. Her collection of textiles and papers is housed in the History Division of the San Bernadino County Museum in California.

Tidball Monographs and the Campers

Harriet Colburn Tidball (1909–69), who grew up in Ypsilanti and later lived in Lansing, was a prominent weaving educator and writer and became a major influence in the Michigan handweaving community. When Tidball took over the Shuttle-Craft Guild, she changed its direction to meet the needs of the times: the yearly subscription covered three monographs, a portfolio of swatches if desired, and three bulletins.[15] Although she became owner of the guild in 1946, she is perhaps best known for her series of twenty-eight weaving monographs of thirty to forty pages each. Most were written during the 1960s and covered weaving topics in great detail, with diagrams, illustrations, instructions, and woven samples in the portfolio editions. In a 1962 interview with the *Portland Oregon Reporter*, Tidball spoke of these new ideas: "We must look to the handweaver for fresh inspiration in design . . . I try, in my monographs, to write about weaving ideas that are one jump ahead of the current fashion."[16] The subjects of the monographs include, among others, Peter Collingwood's work, contemporary tapestry, contemporary clothing design, weft twining, textiles from Central America and South America, textile structure and analysis, and a home-study course in twelve lessons. Some of the monographs are still available.

Like Atwater, Tidball corresponded widely with other weavers. She was first to host Finnish tapestry weaver Eva Anttila[17] and English rug weaver and author Peter Collingwood[18] on their teaching tours in the United States, later writing about their work in her monographs. Anttila taught sixty weavers in tapestry workshops in Hartland, Michigan, and Boulder, Montana, during the summer of 1964. She was "impressed with the eagerness of the American [nonprofessional] weavers to learn."[19] Tidball also invited Swedish author and weaver Malin Selander and others to share their expertise with Michigan weavers anxious to learn.[20] These contemporary weavers emphasized using new colors and creating individual designs instead of "recipe weaving."

Tidball was an avid traveler, and while on a visit to Japan, she contacted Nobuko Kajitani, one of her subscribers in Tokyo. She invited Kajitani to study and work with her in Michigan in 1964. The young woman was a trained weaver in the Bauhaus tradition, and she helped Tidball with her collection and samples for several months before taking a job in textile restoration. In 1966, Kajitani was the first textile conservation restorer hired by the Metropolitan Museum of Art, and she became their chief conservator of textiles, working there for thirty-seven years until her retirement in 2003.[21]

Tidball graduated from Oberlin College with a degree in geology. While working in Columbus, Ohio, in the 1930s, she had taken a night class in weaving at Ohio State University, where she first learned about Atwater. Tidball moved to Montana in 1938 with her first husband, who was on the faculty at Montana State College. There, she met Atwater. This launched Tidball on a lifelong career of weaving and publishing. Her weaving was mostly for experimentation and the working out of patterns for her writing, including *The Weaver's Book* (1961), her monographs, and magazine articles. When Tidball moved briefly to California, she sold the Shuttle-Craft Guild to Mary E. Black, but she regained it in 1960, when she made her headquarters in Lansing. Mary Sayler of Grand Rapids, who studied with Tidball as a member of a group called the Gampers, said that of all her

Harriet Tidball and artist-weaver Peter Collingwood of England, 1962. (Photo courtesy of William Colburn.)

teachers, "Harriet pushed me good." But her "personal memories are of a great companion and friend with a wonderful sense of humor." Sayler wove many of Tidball's samples for the portfolios and used the money she earned to travel with Tidball to weaving centers in Central America and South America.[22] Tidball developed a textile collection of about eight hundred historic, ethnic, and contemporary pieces that she bought on her travels and the swatches woven for the monographs by students, friends, and study groups. When she died in 1969, her large collection of textiles, books, and papers went to the Costume and Textile Study Center in the School of Home Economics at the University of Washington in Seattle.[23] By this time, there were national monthly magazines serving the field: *Craft Horizons* (1950), *Handweaver and Craftsman* (1950), and *Shuttle Spindle and Dyepot* (1969). With Tidball's death, the publication of the *Shuttle-Craft Bulletin* ceased, but the publication of the monographs and books she and Atwater had written continue under the name of Shuttle-Craft Books and are for sale through this company in Coupeville, Washington.

Tidball is a bridge between Mary Atwater and the modern handweaver. She brought to Michigan new ideas and people—artist-weavers whom she met in her travels throughout Europe. She featured the work of local weavers, such as Rosalind "Roz" Berlin, a Michigan State University graduate student teaching at Delta College, and Tonya Rhodes, who taught design at Western Michigan University in Kalamazoo.[24] Tidball's energy and ideas invigorated the fledgling Michigan League of Handweavers (MLH). In 1965, she coordinated its conference in Grand Rapids. Her innovations there set the pattern for the future: a conference theme, room shows, and workshops following the conference. Tidball was active in many organizations and boards, such as the Michigan Craftsmen's Council and the Board of Advisors Fernwood (today Fernwood Botanical Garden and Nature Preserve), consulting and teaching workshops at home and abroad, yet she found time between these and her writing activities to correspond widely, as well as form and work with the Gampers.

The Gampers (who added "Textile Explorers" to their name) were a special study group of twelve multiple-harness weavers from across southern Michigan and regions of Ontario, Canada. Mary Sayler recalls the formation of this very select group of twelve, which she was asked by Tidball to join: "She [Tidball] had certain specifications. She didn't want more than twelve because that would be too many. And less than twelve weren't enough. So we had twelve!"[25] The group was the outgrowth of a ten-day seminar held in April 1959 at Hartland, Michigan; assembled by Ayliffe Ochs, owner of Hartland Area Crafts (formerly Cromaine Crafts); and instructed by Harriet Tidball. This enthusiastic group met for full-day meetings originally once a month and later five times a year. They also held two- and three-day workshops, inviting weaving authorities—such as Malin Selander and Mary Alice Smith, editor of *Handweaver and Craftsman*—as special workshop leaders.[26] The Gampers were an active and serious study group, joining such organizations as the American Crafts Council, and were a major force in promoting the aims of the MLH. Elizabeth Clark of the Weavers Guild of Kalamazoo maintained: "the Gampers were the core of MLH at the time and . . . the energy that drove MLH. They certainly were the creative energy, and also just the spunk. A lot of spunk! They were really a fun bunch of ladies."[27] In 1965, the Gampers hosted the MLH conference in Grand Rapids. They decided their study project for 1964–65 would be supplementary warp. Each member wove an orange hostess dress with white embellishments for the conference (member Libby Crawford wove three!). This study resulted in Tidball's seventeenth monograph, *Supplementary Warp Patterning*, which includes photographs of each Gamper modeling her dress.

In October 1968, the Gampers were the featured presenters at ExCo '68, the Ontario Handweavers and Spinners fourteenth annual conference. It was held in Scarborough, Ontario, at the Guild Inn. The Gampers shared their requirements for a successful study group: to learn and share with others of similar interests—often traveling as far as two hundred miles to meetings to exchange ideas and weaving samples—and benefit from each other's constructive criticism. They said: "When we, as a group, joined the American Craftsmen Council, we felt we needed to add something to our name that at least identified [our] craft . . . Hence: *Textile Explorers* . . . a name that forced us to reach and grow; in fact to dream the impossible dream and to weave the impossible weave. So fantastic has been the impact of a simple thing like a name (Textile Explorers) that in the last international publicity release concerning our group we were, indeed, called 'the outstanding study group in the United States.'" The ExCo '68 brochure lists members at that time: Norie Blakely, Detroit; Mildred Dexter, East Lansing; Renah Green, Grand Blanc; Harriet Tidball, Lansing; Eunice Anders, Leamington, Ontario; Ethel Alexander, Grand Ledge; Marge Anderson, Detroit; Libby Crawford, Detroit; Faithe Nunneley, Minneapolis, Minnesota; Mary Sayler, Grand Rapids; Lillian Serpa, Birmingham; and Madeleine Smith, Windsor, Ontario. Blakely, Dexter, Green, and Tidball were original members.[28]

The early work of Mary Atwater, continued by Tidball, laid the foundation for a growing network of handweaving guilds across America. Women and some men were finding weaving to be a useful and creative activity. The middle class was growing, and more people had leisure time and disposable income. New weavers learned through books, magazines, or classes. They found others with similar interests and expertise and banded together. A growing appreciation of handicrafts encouraged exhibits and sales. With this increased energy came more local yarn supply shops, community art centers, helpful instruction in newsletters and craft magazines, and traveling "stars"—with special and new expertise—who gave workshops.

THREE

Hartland

An Ideal Crafts Community

Communities play an important role in the revival and promotion of weaving, through education, facilities, financial support, and exhibitions. Usually, these community efforts are the result of the shared work of many individuals, but in the case of Hartland, it is the story of one man with an ideal and a dream.

J. Robert Crouse Sr. returned to his boyhood home of Hartland when he retired in 1928 from a successful Ohio electric and lighting business. His Hartland Area Project, formally proposed in 1931, was a social experiment to create an ideal rural community and constructive social environment.[1] There would be a village center with good schools, music, drama, handicrafts, library service, and health and welfare services. Hartland was located in southern Michigan, on old U.S. Route 23, north of Ann Arbor. A few miles to the south, Crouse had already built the Waldenwoods conference center (in 1924–25), where business, educational, recreational, religious, and creative groups could host conferences in an idyllic setting by a small lake in the woods. Today, the center is often used for banquets and wedding receptions.

Crouse purchased the Hartland Grist Mill and renovated it in 1934 to serve as a first home for Cromaine Crafts, the heart of his new village. The center quickly outgrew the space and moved into a hundred-year-old tavern on Avon Street, which became the weaving center's home for the next forty years. During this era, hundreds of weavers and shoppers visited the center. Handwoven tea towels, place mats, blankets, and runners by the Hartland weavers were sold in over two hundred retail outlets in the nation.[2] Hartland was one of the largest producers of handwoven fabrics in the United States outside Appalachia in the 1930s and 1940s.[3]

When Crouse decided to establish the craft center, he hired Osma (Palmer) Couch (later Gallinger) from Suffern, New York, where she had

Cromaine Crafts building, Hartland, Michigan, ca. 1935. (Photo courtesy of the Hartland Area Historical Society.)

Linen and cotton hand towels and table runners labeled "Hand-made by Cromaine" or "Handwoven HARTLAND AREA CRAFTS Michigan," 1930s and 1940s. (Photo by Marie A. Gile.)

established a reputation as a teacher of weaving and as a writer. Her task was to create a center for "things useful and beautiful" through skillful and earnest effort of talented hands. Cromaine Crafts would become known for its products of high quality and its dedication to teaching profitable skills to children and adults in the community.

Not long after opening the workshop, furniture designer and producer Milo Gallinger and the two original woodworkers from Hartland Grist Mill, Jack and Abner Guernsey, designed and built the Cromaine looms, which were sold widely in these years. Cromaine Crafts grew rapidly. In 1935, two experienced weavers from Berea, Kentucky, were hired to teach and weave. Also joining the staff was Swedish weaver and handspinner Mrs. Martina Lindahl of Plainwell, Michigan, of whom it was said that "the only thing she can't spin is peach fuzz."[4] She developed custom variations in weave patterns, called Whig Rose, Honeysuckle, and Swedish Lace. Osma Couch and Milo Gallinger married, and Mrs. Lindahl and her son Clifford lived with them at first.

Katherine Lindahl recalls the workshop's early years: "My mother would open the craft shop on a Sunday afternoon. She'd work six days a week. In the summertime, under the walnut tree, we had a platform out there and I'd sit out . . . and weave rugs. There would be cars lined up [from] one end of town to the other . . . [to] come to see the Cromaine Crafts."[5] Their business grew so quickly that in 1936 a branch of the Cromaine Craft Center was opened in Howell (referred to as Cromaine Crafts of Howell and in 1939 reorganized to Creative Crafts of Howell). Both Gallinger and Lindahl taught many to weave and spin and made countless friends during their years of teaching and running the shop. Jo Graham, a charter member of the Michigan League of Handweavers, recalled that Osma Gallinger "proved to be a competent teacher." In 1934, Graham took "a [one-week] crash course" with Gallinger to qualify her to become the weaving teacher at Grant, Michigan.[6] Muriel Neeland, a Latin teacher from Mancelona, remembered her first trip to Hartland: "Mrs. Gallinger took me to another weaver's house to stay overnight and get my breakfast. We had to come down to the corner and go, I believe it was a half a mile, and then over to the middle of the next block. But it was along in the fall—rather late fall. It was so nice . . . then I had my breakfast, and I walked [to the shop] . . . and I had my other two meals with Mrs. Gallinger. She took me back to this woman's house at night . . . I wove all day. And she let me weave all evening! . . . I could pick out the colors I wanted and treadle the way I wanted to . . . Then I did a linen towel, I think it was, with lace weaves. Oh, I was thrilled to pieces with it all!"[7] Neeland also could not leave for home without a loom for herself: "I ordered a loom from Mr. Gallinger. And I remember when it came to town . . . My husband said it created quite a sensation downtown. Everyone wondered about it, you know. But the man brought it up here and we got it in. I was glad to have it."[8]

During the early years at Cromaine Crafts, Mary Atwater's efforts with the Shuttle-Craft Guild were well known, and several weaving guilds had been founded in American cities and rural areas. The idea of holding the National Weaving Institute at Waldenwoods in June 1938 was a natural outgrowth of the Waldenwoods conference philosophy. Gallinger and Crouse would organize an institute that would meet annually in a peaceful, natural setting that would refresh and energize the participants, and offer opportunities for teachers and students to meet together and learn and develop ways to promote weaving. It would excite interest in weaving in Michigan by bringing in national figures. Mary Meigs Atwater was the featured speaker and instructor for the first institute and for many that followed.

For the first institute, Mrs. Atwater conducted two two-week sessions at Waldenwoods, where the participants engaged in sampling twenty

A young student weaving in the Cromaine Crafts weaving studio, 1935. (Photo by the *Detroit Free Press*. Courtesy of the Walter P. Reuther Library, Wayne State University.)

different patterns. They made a day trip to Cranbrook Academy of Art and Greenfield Village.[9] A number of institutes, weaving conferences, workshops, and meetings were held in the years following. At these early institutes, weaving was for everyone, at a moderate price. "For the first two weeks session," Ruth Cross said, "the fee was $40.00, [which] included board, room, and tuition."[10]

Mary Black, author of *Key to Weaving* (1945), was director of occupational therapy at Ypsilanti State Hospital from 1932 to 1939. She attended and lectured on "The Theraputics of Weaving" at the first conference. Black was inspired to write her own book based on the simplified explanations she had developed for her patients while working in Ypsilanti.[11] Mary Atwater and Harriet Tidball also worked as occupational therapists: Atwater worked with World War I veterans, beginning in 1918; both Atwater and Tidball worked with World War II veterans. Tidball would travel from her home in Bozeman, Montana, to work with patients in Basin, where Atwater lived; while there, she would stop to visit Atwater.[12]

The growth of Cromaine Crafts created a need for restructuring the business. The Gallingers took over selling looms. Osma directed the facility, which included weaving, consulting, writing books and publicity to promote Hartland's handwoven crafts nationally, and managing the annual institute. The Cromaine Craft Center operated under the new name of Hartland Area Crafts. Mrs. Lindahl managed the craft center's gift shop, as well as conducting weaving, teaching and selling. A studio of fine art and an area craft museum were headed by others. During this time, the Lindahls moved into their own home in town, where Clifford Lindahl recalls demonstrating weaving every Saturday on a platform near the roadside, doing his bit to attract the tourists.[13] In 1944, the Gallingers moved to Pennsylvania, and the many local weavers who had made Cromaine Crafts their center met as a guild in order to keep up their regular association. Weaving continued at the Hartland Area Craft Shop, and sales were still strong, but the looms were no longer produced. In 1946, when Clifford Lindahl returned home from military service in World War II, Mr. Crouse asked him to start building looms. He developed one according to his mother's design, and they were sold until 1959. Mrs. Lindahl retired officially in 1951, and although others managed the shop, she continued to weave and spin. She was ninety-five years old when she died in 1975.[14]

When the craft shop was sold to Ayliffe Ochs in 1957, activities were revived at Hartland. Detroit guilds and weavers came for classes and meetings. Although the heyday of weaving production had passed for that town, the Ochs—new owners of the Cromaine/Hartland Area Craft Shop—had infused it with new energy. In November 1958, the shop was featured nationally in the weaving magazine *Warp and Weft*.[15] Throughout the fall of 1958 and spring of 1959, a small group of weavers representing several of the guilds in the region met in Ochs's office to discuss formation of a statewide association. The first conference was held on July 24, 1959, and the Michigan League of Handweavers became a reality. The 135 attendees enthusiastically supported its founding. The MLH drew weavers once again to conferences held at Waldenwoods in the early 1960s.[16] Black Sheep Weavers, a guild that meets today, carries on the tradition of this weaving center into the new century, with workshops, seminars, and exhibits.

FOUR

Arts and Crafts

Cranbrook and the
College for Creative Studies

Michigan embraced the Arts and Crafts movement, associated with the late nineteenth-century social reformer William Morris, who publicized the ideals of fine craft work through lectures, journal articles, and the products of his craft workshops. The movement grew in reaction to the Industrial Revolution. It promoted work artfully crafted by trained and creative hands. Beauty, simplicity, and craftsmanship in useful objects were valued and thought to improve the quality of everyday life—in contrast to mass-produced factory goods. Boston formed the first arts and crafts society in the United States, in 1897. Twenty other cities quickly followed, including Grand Rapids, Michigan, in 1902. The Detroit Society of Arts and Crafts formed in 1906.[1] These societies held craft and design exhibitions to promote their ideals and began to hold craft classes. Another, later influence came from the German Bauhaus movement, founded in 1919 by Walter Gropius at Weimar. It brought artists and craftspeople together in order to create better designs for mass-produced, industrial products as well as individual works. The Arts and Crafts and Bauhaus ideals influenced both formal art education and the handicraft revival in Michigan, in such places as Cranbrook Academy of Art (founded in 1925, just north of Detroit, in Bloomfield Hills), the rural handicraft community at Hartland (founded in 1931, north of Brighton), Greenfield Village, and the College for Creative Studies, which grew out of efforts by the Detroit Society of Arts and Crafts (1926).

In the early twentieth century, Detroit was growing rapidly as a dynamic urban center, with modern architecture, decorative arts, theater, fashionable homes, and impressive commercial and civic structures. It was also a city of immigrants from abroad and citizens from elsewhere in the United States—people with skills in engineering, crafts, and design, as well as common laborers seeking better wages and a better life. Between 1906 and 1931, the Detroit Society of Arts and Crafts (DSAC) brought to the city works by almost every major craftsperson active in Europe and America.[2] The DSAC's shop provided an important local outlet for the work of its members until it closed in 1931. The DSAC's design school taught informal classes in painting, sculpture, metalwork, ceramics, and textiles and held local exhibitions. Together, the DSAC and the Detroit Institute of Arts (DIA) served as a focus for the development of arts and crafts in urban Detroit and intended to elevate the public taste. The school later grew into an accredited arts college. Many leading citizens were involved in founding these art organizations; George C. Booth, who headed the *Detroit News*, was the DSAC's first president and a founder. One of the exhibits the DSAC brought to Detroit was the 1927 exhibit of Swedish decorative arts. Sweden was a recognized leader in contemporary design, architecture, and the applied arts.

George C. Booth was involved in promoting art education through the DSAC, and he had been studying about other schools of industry and applied arts. In 1927 he included an arts and crafts school in his plans for Cranbrook Academy to be built on the grounds of his extensive estate in Bloomfield Hills, just north of the city. Through his contacts at the University of Michigan in Ann Arbor, where his son was an architectural student, he met visiting professor Eliel Saarinen, a noted Finnish architect. Together, they envisioned not an art school in the ordinary meaning but a place where master artists would work together to provide "self-education under good leadership." Saarinen was not interested in returning to medieval craftsmanship; rather, he envisioned a school to develop designers for contemporary life.[3]

Cranbrook Educational Community

Over a period of years, from 1925 through 1942, Booth and Saarinen worked together to create the Cranbrook educational community, consisting of Cranbrook Academy of Art, a school for boys and the Kingswood School for girls, an elementary school, an institute of science, a library, and a museum. First built were the early art buildings, where Saarinen had his drafting studio, and the school for boys (1925). These buildings are west of the entrance from Lone Pine Road. By 1928, the craft studios and residences for the master craftspeople and students were going up across the street. Cranbrook Academy of Art was officially opened in 1932. A landscaped area with a long reflecting pool containing statues by Carl Milles and a wide staircase led to the library and museum (1937–42). Today's new craft studio building is just behind the museum. The science buildings, girls' school, and elementary school are located farther back on the extensive grounds.

The basement weaving studio at Studio Loja Saarinen, May 1935. *Left to right:* Elizabeth Edmark, Marie Bexell (wife of John Bexell, who built the Cranbrook loom for Loja Saarinen), Peggy Buckbourough, and Gerda Nyberg. (Photo courtesy of Cranbrook Archives, no. 2744.)

Saarinen was named president and head of the architecture program. His wife, artist Loja Saarinen, established her own weaving studio and the school's first weaving classes. She had a degree in art from the Finnish Academy of Art in Helsinki, with specialization in sculpture, photography, and model building. When Henry Booth asked her if they should order textiles and rugs from Finland to go with her husband's "new buildings and furnishings," she said, "Why not weave them here?" Booth agreed; thus, most of the weaving in her studio those first years was created for specific spaces in the school buildings.[4] In 1929, she hired Maja Wirde from the Handarbetets Vänner (The Association of Friends of Textile Art) School in Stockholm. Lillian Holm and Ruth Ingvarson, who studied tapestry and rug weaving at the Märta Måås Fjetterström studio in Båstad, Sweden, joined Saarinen's studio in 1929–30. Most of the twenty weavers who worked part-time at the studio were Swedish weavers who lived in Detroit. The studio was organized on the European model: the artists designed, and the weavers wove. Wirde and Holm did design some of the Cranbrook tapestries and rugs, but most were designed by the Saarinens. Wirde, Holm, and Ingvarson taught weaving classes in Detroit in addition to their studio work.

Mrs. Saarinen's work was widely exhibited in American art museums, and many originals are still in use at the Kingswood School and in the Cranbrook textile collection. John P. Bexell, a skilled Swedish cabinetmaker and the husband of one of the weavers, was asked to develop a loom for the studio's custom work. In 1936, he made the first Bexell loom, later called the Cranbrook loom, which he produced until 1977, when he sold the business.[5] In 1933, Holm became the first full-time weaving teacher at the Kingswood School. She lived in a former ballroom on the top floor of the girls' school until her retirement in 1965.[6] Her tapestries won prizes in local competitions, and some are displayed in the school lobby.

Weaving is still taught at the girls school, in the original spacious studio, with many of the early looms. Tapestry artist Lois Bryant was amazed to find looms in their same places in 2004 when she returned for a thirtieth-anniversary class reunion. Students took a variety of arts courses from seventh grade on, including metalwork, jewelry, ceramics, painting, sculpture, and weaving. At the tenth-grade level, weaving became an elective, and Bryant continued weaving through her senior year. The 1970s class was project-oriented—making pillows, rugs, purses, and rya rugs. Students explored the latest techniques, often instructed by teachers from the fiber department at Cranbrook Academy of Art (CAA), including Robert L. Kidd. Bryant continued her art education at Brown University and Rhode Island School of Design and specializes in tapestry commissions.[7]

Design for Industry

Loja Saarinen's studio was closed in 1942, when she retired due to the war and a lack of orders. Marianne Strengell, another Swedish-speaking Finn and friend of the Saarinens who had been teaching the weaving classes, became director of the weaving department at CAA, a job she held from 1942 to 1961. Strengell was known for her industrial designs. The CAA weaving studio was still in the art building adjacent to the main gate and reflecting pool in 1950, when Jack Lenor Larsen was a student studying with Strengell. A large open room was used for meetings and for preparing warps and finishing large rugs. Behind that was a workshop with two dozen Cranbrook looms, the fly-shuttle power-loom room, and Strengell's studio. The dye room was located in the lower level.[8]

Strengell received many commissions for design work, interiors, and woven and printed textiles—including all the textiles for Manhattan House and the Terrace Plaza Hotel in Cincinnati and rugs for the General Motors Technical Center. She designed fabrics for Ford Motor Company, General Motors, Chrysler, American Motors, and United Airlines. She also designed for Knoll Associates, a designer of furniture and interiors. Strengell had

Fabric samples (front and back) of synthetic fibers assembled using a partial compound satin weave, designed by Marianne Strengell for use in automobiles and manufactured by Chatham Manufacturing, ca. 1956. Strengell was consultant to Chatham Manufacturing from 1954 to 1960. Also by Strengell is the center sample of natural fibers and grasses. (Photo by Pearl Yee Wong. Courtesy of Michigan State University Museum.)

over seventy solo exhibitions, and her work is in many museum collections. She was an expert on fiber analysis and explored many new fibers—metallic, synthetic, fiberglass, and plastic—to find out what they could do in fabrics. On an assignment for the government in 1951, she analyzed textile possibilities for native plants in the Philippines.[9]

Strengell encouraged her students to stay away from the library, to get to know themselves and what they had to offer—to find their own creativity.

Robert Sailors and Marianne Strengell, *at left*, in the Cranbrook weaving studio, January 1944. (Photo courtesy of Cranbrook Archives, no. 6513.)

She experimented with new materials and expected them to do the same. She told them to play with yarns and colors and textures in as many combinations as possible. As the department focus was on design for industry and architectural projects, Strengell insisted that the students work within limitations: price range, raw materials, available labor, equipment, dyes, climate. Her students had to know the existing conditions before solving a design problem.[10] She trained some extraordinarily talented students who became leaders in the field: Jack Lenor Larsen, Robert Sailors, Robert L. Kidd, Olga de Amaral, Ed Rossbach, and Nelly Sethna of India. Sailors, who became Strengell's assistant and taught the use of the power loom at CAA under her direction, established his own design studio in 1947 in Bitley, near his hometown of Grand Rapids, Michigan, weaving for architects and interior designers. He developed innovative woven window shades and sculptural hangings and fabrics made with uncommon materials.[11]

Strengell continued designing after leaving CAA. She died in 1998 at age eighty-eight. Her archives are at CAA and at the Archives of American Art at the Smithsonian Institution in Washington, DC. After Strengell left, weaving at CAA turned more toward free experimentation and personal vision in fiber art.

Marianne Strengell's leadership at CAA was followed by a series of distinguished artist-weavers: Glen Kaufmann (1962–67), Meda Parker Johnson (1967–68), Robert L. Kidd (1968–70), Gerhardt Knodel (1970–96), and Jane Lackey (1997–). Each brought individual talents to their artwork and teaching. Their appointments also reflected a change in direction for this prestigious graduate art school—from a focus on design for living, architecture, and industry to an emphasis on the fine arts. Since 1942, most students have written a thesis to graduate with an MFA.[12]

Gerhardt Knodel, artist-in-residence and head of the fiber department at CAA from 1970 through 1996, grew up on the West Coast. He focused on art and theater in high school and studied art at the University of California, Los Angeles, where he received an MFA. In the 1960s, he taught at the high school level and developed his own studio work in weaving. Knodel has noted of that time: "Textiles were an area that offered the exotic—Peru, Afghanistan, all over the world. Textiles were being discovered." During Knodel's student days, weaving instruction was permeated by Cranbrook Academy of Art and the Bauhaus approach. Trude Guermonprez, who studied at the Bauhaus and went first to Black Mountain College, where Anni and Josef Albers taught, later came to California College of Arts and Crafts. Knodel acknowledged: "She was in northern California and there were some Cranbrook Academy people in southern California. They set the pace for the way weaving was to be explored." Knodel explained that structure and function came first: "The idea of art textiles barely existed." But in the 1960s, the idea of textile wall art was emerging. Knodel noted, "The rya rug was the place to make *the* art statement."[13] Knodel had seen early space hangings and watched students from the Haystack Mountain School of Crafts in Maine shaping weavings on the loom. That set in motion his own exploration of flexible textile environments.

When Knodel arrived at Cranbrook in Bloomfield Hills in 1970, the students were in strong revolt against tapestry as the only form of weaving considered art. They had seen the new shows at the Museum of Modern Art that introduced significant new ideas in art fabric and sculptural fiber, and Knodel oriented the program to the fine arts. "It's not about training people to go into industry. It's training people how to produce something that is expressive, something that is individual and unique in relationship to the broader definition of art," he explained in a recent interview.[14]

The CAA fiber department was already moving away from its industry orientation and toward fine art. Glen Kaufman and Robert L. Kidd had introduced rya (tufted) works and sculptural fiber-art pieces. Novelty fibers, such as wood and metal slats, were popularized by Cranbrook artist Robert

Sailors. The California colors and metallics associated with the work of Dorothy Liebes could now be seen in CAA studios. As Knodel has claimed, the Museum of Modern Art's show of art fabric by Mildred Constantine and Jack Lenor Larsen in 1968–69 and the publication of their book *Beyond Craft* (1973) were "very significant in showing the new ideas." Postwar work in Poland, where fiber works became sculptural, encouraged Knodel's own thinking about creating fiber environments.[15] Developed under Knodel's direction was a process of studio critique in which broad-based conceptual positions assisted students to build a dialogue about their work and its relationships to other fields of art. Knodel also taught courses in the history of textiles, to encourage discovery of aesthetic and conceptual resources as the underpinnings of new work. The development of his own architecturally scaled work for major sites across the United States presented students with new possibilities for projecting their innovative visions into the world in imaginative ways.[16]

Jane Lackey, artist-in-residence and head of the fiber department since 1997, when Knodel became director of CAA, carries on in that spirit. She studied at California College of Arts and Crafts (now California College of the Arts) with Guermonprez, where she wove and dyed in ikat, using weaving as a kind of drawing. After completing a master's degree at CAA in 1979, Lackey went to Kansas City Art Institute, where she was professor and chair of the fiber program. There, she was instrumental in establishing a nationally recognized, broadly based undergraduate fiber program. Her

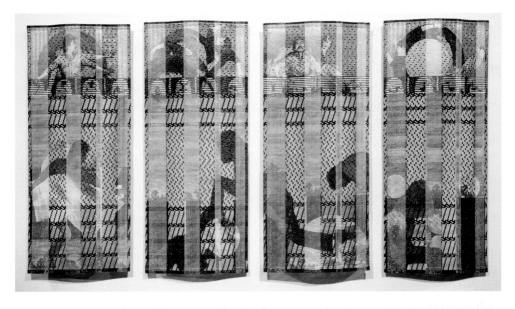

Guardians of the New Day, four handwoven panels of cotton, linen, and mylar by Gerhardt Knodel, 1987. (Photo courtesy of Gerhardt Knodel.)

FASCINATION WITH FIBER

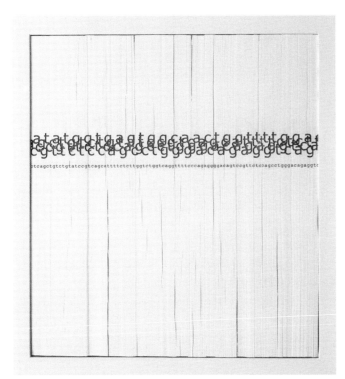

stanza 3 by Jane Lackey of Cranbrook Academy of Art, 2003. This piece is made from dictionaries, gesso, and laser engravings and framed in lacquered wood. (Photo by Tim Thayer. Courtesy of Jane Lackey.)

current abstract fiber pieces—using felting, painted surfaces, and paper—explore invisible information (such as the codes that run digital systems or the human genome) and comment on the human condition.

Lackey points out that students who come to the fiber program at CAA often have worked in some aspect of textiles and have diverse interests and educational backgrounds. So the character of each group of seven or eight students admitted to the new two-year program changes each year. The goal remains as from the beginning—to encourage individual development through cerebral and studio work. Each student is individually advised by Lackey and develops a study plan for the two years. All students in the fiber program attend weekly seminars and critiques and meet individually with the artist-in-residence and visiting artists. They write papers on fiber issues, an artist statement, and a thesis. Graduating students present their work at the Cranbrook Museum each spring. Students use the summers to develop skills related to their research and for studio practice.[17] Fiber, metal, and ceramics share a new building on the CAA campus, with specially equipped labs and studios. Each student has a studio alcove and the run of the dye lab, darkroom, computer, printing, and weaving studios. Students have previous expertise in fiber arts and may bring their own specialized tools, such as sewing or knitting machines. Their interests run the gamut of contemporary techniques in fiber arts.

The College for Creative Studies

The College for Creative Studies in Detroit owes its origin to the Detroit Society of Arts and Crafts, which wanted to bring training and education in industrial design to Detroit. The DSAC founded Detroit School of Design in 1911, but that school failed in 1918 for lack of support. The DSAC also offered informal classes and art competitions for students in the city's public schools. Finally, after noticing the lack of crafts and applied arts in shows it sponsored, the group established the Art School of the Detroit Society of Arts and Crafts in 1926. Leading artists, craftspeople, and designers were brought in as faculty, but for some years, the focus was on instruction in fine arts. In 1936, Jay Boorsma, a commercial artist with a background in fine arts, became director of the school, and he made efforts to strengthen industrial art and design education. World War II had created a decline in enrollments, but returning GIs enrolled and allowed the school to grow and prosper. Its director, Sarkis Sarkisian, encouraged individuality and craftsmanship and opened the school to all races and national groups. Black students, including veterans, who were unwelcome at many schools, found this art school a place to develop their talents. In 1958, the school commissioned Minoru Yamasaki and Associates to design a new building for the craft workshops and began moving toward accreditation. In 1977, the school was renamed the Center for Creative Studies—College of Art and Design and was one of three accredited art schools in Michigan. It offers a BFA in eight departments: animation and digital media, communication design, crafts, fine arts, illustration, industrial design, interior design, and photography.[18] In 2001, it became the College for Creative Studies, with 208 faculty members and a larger campus to accommodate its growing size and importance in the city's cultural center.

The school's first weaving program was started in 1949 by Ruth Ingvarson, who came to the school with Swedish education in weaving and experience at the Saarinen studio at Cranbrook. She went on to develop a weaving course at Wayne State University in 1952, when weaving stopped at the DSAC school. Weaving continued at Wayne State in the 1960s, with a succession of Cranbrook Art Academy graduates as weaving teachers (Eleen Auvil, Marilyn Leon, and Urban Jupena, who added surface design). Susan Aaron-Taylor (a CAA graduate) was hired to head the fiber-design section of the crafts department in 1973. Mollie Fletcher (a CAA graduate) joined the Center for Creative Studies in 1980 to teach weaving; in 1986, Sue Moran, a University of Michigan graduate, joined to teach surface design. Aaron-Taylor, the college's only full-time faculty member, has taught a wide range of fiber courses, from weaving to mixed media.[19] Before specializing, each student takes foundation courses in art and a series of short courses covering the range of processes and techniques. A BFA in crafts with a fibers specialization is offered. Fletcher teaches the weaving classes and puts her

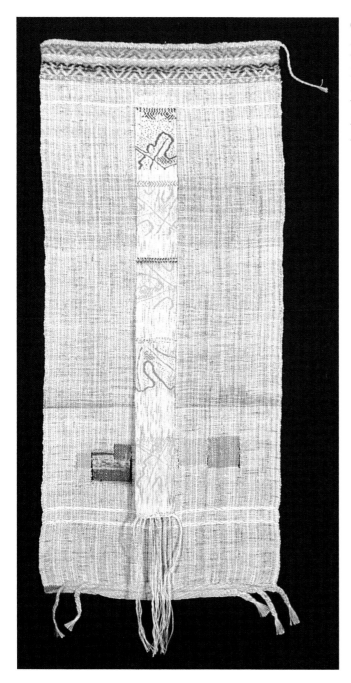

Glimpse, a wall hanging of handpicked brocade, tapestry, twills, and braiding by Mollie H. Fletcher, College of Creative Studies, 2004. (Photo by Pearl Yee Wong. Courtesy of the Michigan State University Museum.)

students through a series of exercises designed to cover setting up the four-shaft loom, weave structures, color and texture, and special techniques, such as woven *shibori* (Japanese shaped resist dyeing) or bleach-out on weaving. The intermediate and advanced weaving classes are run as independent studies, with each student developing a plan and presenting work for critique every four weeks. Each student has a senior show. Fiber students may choose to focus on weaving, surface, or mixed media/sculpture.

Much of the excitement in fibers during the 1990s has been in developing new surface treatment techniques and in applying the computer and digitized images. But Mollie Fletcher believes that "pushing the boundaries" is still possible within the "traditional" parameters of weaving. She argues that weavers should explore the new materials and combinations of materials, new dye and chemical processes, finishing and shrinking techniques, and flat (versus three-dimensional) surfaces. She maintains that they should also explore sources of inspiration and the use of imagery in designs.[20] Fletcher specializes in tapestries, often designed for public buildings, such as her heartwarming scene of flowers and butterflies at Detroit's Beaumont Hospital.

Detroit is an urban center with auto manufacturing, communications, and service industries needing skilled designers. Students still have these interests. Art schools that began early in the twentieth century, when Arts and Crafts and Bauhaus ideals were salient, have today changed to meet contemporary needs. But the demands of excellence in craftsmanship and promotion of individual creativity remain central at these schools, where future artists, designers, and teachers explore and express their culture in their own ways.

FIVE

Guilds and Groups
The Grassroots Movement

The guild movement has kept the craft of weaving alive and open to new ideas nationally and globally. Local and regional guilds of handweavers began forming early in the twentieth century, when clusters of new weavers banded together to share their knowledge and offer help. Boston's guild (1922) is generally considered the first original U.S. guild, but guilds formed on both coasts and in the Midwest prior to World War II. After the war, many more guilds formed. With them came visiting workshop teachers, traveling exhibits, national meetings, institutes and conferences, national magazines, and high standards of performance.

The medieval textile guilds of professional craftsmen set terms, conditions, and entrance standards. The modern handicraft guild carries along some of these ideals, but they are neither binding nor restrictive of entry. When Mary Atwater adopted the term *guild* in naming her Shuttle-Craft Guild, she focused on "insistence on a high standard of workmanship." She explained that it was a proud honor to be admitted to a guild and that it required long apprenticeship and mastery. But there was too much secrecy and envy. Atwater insisted that the new guilds should be used to promote sharing of information and help to others interested in the craft.[1] Modern handweaving guilds support these ideals. Early in their development, many guilds required submission of acceptable work for admission. Later, some guilds opened to all the fiber arts and often made jurying of works, put before the public for sale or exhibition, the means to sustain a standard of excellence.

Early Michigan Guilds

Guilds in Michigan began forming primarily during and after World War II. There was growing interest in crafts, and more places to learn how to weave emerged: schools, arts and crafts centers, YWCAs, and home economics and art education classes. Atwater's institutes, later called conferences, helped spread the knowledge, as did her publications. Guilds were organized through friendships, associations with yarn shops, museums, art associations, and craft bazaars—and by dedicated teachers who offered their energy and expertise.

One of the earliest known Michigan guilds dates from 1937: the Livingston County Weavers Guild formed in May of that year. Over two hundred weavers were a part of this guild, which met formally once a year and also met monthly in close neighborhood groups.[2] Of the thirty-four guilds in the Michigan League of Handweavers (MLH) today, most formed in the 1940s and later. The Blue Pots (1946), which became dormant for a time and revived as the Yarnwinders Fiber Guild (1972) of Marquette, has the longest tradition. The Michigan Weavers Guild of Detroit, the Toledo Area Weavers Guild in Ohio, and the Fort Wayne Weavers Guild in Indiana (known then as the Shuttlecraft Guild) are close behind in their starting date (1947) and have remained in continuous operation. The Detroit Handweavers and Spinners and the Niles Handweavers Guild started in 1948–49. The 1950s and 1960s brought new guilds in Detroit, Lansing, Baldwin, Ann Arbor, Grand Rapids, Kalamazoo, Midland, and Chassell (in the Upper Peninsula's copper country). Over a dozen guilds formed in the 1970s, and a few formed in each decade since then, the most recent being the Lake Charlevoix Area Guild, founded in October 2002. Michigan guilds vary in size from a handful of weavers to a hundred or more. The guilds of the MLH are listed at the back of this book.

All of the MLH guilds hold regular meetings, either in members' homes or in larger public spaces in their communities. Lectures by members or guest speakers focus on topics of current interest in weaving and fiber arts. Most guilds have study groups that will pursue a specific weaving/fiber project or pattern for a period of time and share the results with a display at exchanges or conferences. Sales of work made by members are popular ways of raising money for the guild. Many guilds, especially in areas with sheep and wool-shearing traditions, participate in local history days, annual festivals, and sheep-to-shawl days, where participants shear, spin, and weave a garment within set time limits.[3] Outreach projects aimed at educating the public about handweaving and cloth speak to new generations of weavers. Each guild has its own rich history and special enthusiasms. Guilds come together on a statewide basis in the MLH.

Starting a Guild

Fernwood, a nature center near the city of Niles in southern Michigan, was an active center for weavers between the 1940s and 1970s. Founders Kay

The Blue Pots, ca. 1949–55. *Left to right:* Etta Goos, Catherine Wilkerson, Julia "DeeDee" Tibbitts, unknown, Martha Kallio Johnson, and Kay Holman. (Photo courtesy of the Yarnwinders Fiber Guild.)

and Walter Boydston of Chicago envisioned Fernwood as a place where nature would be a source of inspiration and creativity for the arts and crafts. Kay Boydston and Gladys Kneeshaw met in Niles and formed a friendship through their interest in weaving. They had both lived in Chicago, where they received some weaving instruction. During her retirement in Niles, Kneeshaw had begun operating a bookshop. Learning of Hartland's program, Boydston and Kneeshaw signed up for weaving with Martina Lindahl. Greatly motivated after their experience, they returned to establish the Niles Handweavers Guild. The guild and Fernwood sponsored numerous workshops together and brought nationally and internationally prominent weavers to the site.

Weaving projects and items made in the beguiling woodland setting often used ferns and other nature themes. During 1963–65, the guild investigated natural dyeing ("begun in Esther Lester's garage"), and their research was displayed and published by the Brooklyn Botanical Gardens in 1963–64. *Handweaver and Craftsman* also published their work about natural dyeing, and samples for the project were donated to the Smithsonian textile collection.[4] In 1969, the guild was asked to weave a large wall hanging for the Niles Community Library. After three years of planning and weaving by nineteen members, the hanging was installed at the library during

Sheep-to-shawl competition at the Ella Sharp Museum in Jackson, arranged by the Jackson Handweavers Guild, 1992. *Left to right:* Ginger Watson, Diane Crosley, Donna Craft, Marilyn Kempf, and Alice Gier. (Photo courtesy of the Jackson Handweavers Guild.)

George Good from Michigan State University's Department of Animal Sciences, demonstrates shearing a sheep during the sheep-to-shawl event at the Michigan State University Museum, May 15, 2004. (Photo by Pearl Yee Wong. Courtesy of the Michigan State University Museum.)

a ceremony on October 15, 1973. Today, the Niles Handweavers Guild continues to meet at Fernwood.[5]

Although Fernwood was founded by two women, often a guild forms due to the efforts of one person. In an effort to revive interest in handweaving, Dorothea Buell, who had moved to Chassell in Michigan's Upper

Waiting to be sheared—a sheep from Michigan State University's Sheep Teaching and Research Center visits the grounds of the Michigan State University Museum, May 15, 2004. (Photo by Pearl Yee Wong. Courtesy of the Michigan State University Museum.)

Peninsula, held an open house in November 1963 to introduce the community to her weavings and the twelve looms in her studio. Buell had learned to weave in the 1930s through self-instruction and attending workshops. Over the years, she became a prominent weaver, exhibiting at local, state, and national craft shows, frequently taking top honors. Her open house resulted in eight students, and in June 1964, the first meeting of the new guild, the Portage Overshots, was held. In the following year, the guild changed its name to the Buellwood Weavers Guild, in recognition of Mrs. Buell's untiring efforts and interests. Her efforts did not end with the Buellwood Weavers Guild; she also organized weaving guilds in Amasa, Michigan, and Green Bay, Wisconsin. Buell believed strongly in the guild system, in the MLH, and in the Handweavers Guild of America (HGA). She wrote to the editor of the HGA's *Shuttle Spindle and Dyepot*: "I have been firmly convinced that Guilds and study groups are the finest sort of inspiration any weaver can have; the personal contact a Guild gives far outweighs the help a written dissertation can give."[6] At her death, her guild wrote that they would miss their dear friend and teacher Mrs. Bee (as she was fondly known), who had "contagious enthusiasm and Job-like patience."[7]

Although they never organized as a formal guild, Muriel Neeland and three friends, using the first initial of each of their names, started a group called the LAMMs (most likely during the late 1940s or early 1950s) in the Traverse City–Mancelona region of Michigan's Lower Peninsula. (*Lam* is the name of a part of the loom.) Neeland, from the small rural town of Mancelona, and Loretta Nichols, Alice Tunison, and Margaret Millstein, all from Traverse City (over forty miles away), met in each other's homes to share information about their weaving projects. At the first conference of the MLH in Hartland, Neeland presented the program "Needs of the Isolated Weaver."[8] Neeland and Nichols, charter members of the MLH, were energetic and dedicated weavers, hosting the 1966 MLH conference in Traverse City.

Guilds are often hidden treasures in a community. They are not listed in the phone book and usually have no permanent clubhouse. Their existence is dependent on word of mouth, newspaper notices of events, or publicity through a yarn shop. In fact, the shops often spark development of a new guild. Sharon Huss owned a shop in Grayling and was putting a new

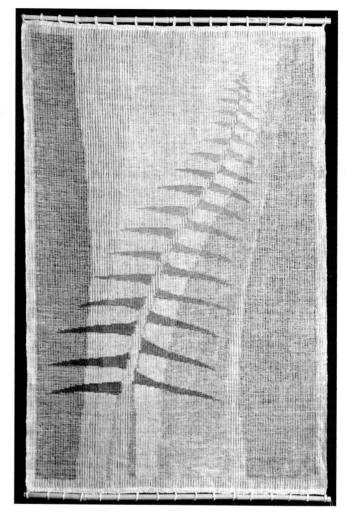

Fern-inspired wall hanging woven by Fernwood weaving workshop teacher Theo Moorman of England, ca. 1960s–1970s. (Photo by Pearl Yee Wong. Courtesy of the Michigan State University Museum.)

warp on her loom when Bobbie Katkuhn and Rosemary Malbin visited the shop. They stayed to help and became intrigued with weaving. In June 1990, Sharon held a tea to organize a new guild, the AuSable Manistee Fiber Guild. Sometimes, guilds are inspired by an initial spark of interest. This happened when Rita Kent, who moved her weaving business to Mount Morris Township in Genesee County in the fall of 1976, suggested the guild idea to local weavers who came to her shop to buy supplies. Shortly after, the weavers organized a guild, with nine members. The Eastside Hand-weavers Guild formed in September 1975 and met at the Needles and Knots knitting supply shop in Grosse Pointe Woods until the group grew too large. Today, members meet at the Children's Home on Crook Road in Grosse Pointe Woods and have study groups for weave structures and for spinning.[9] In Saginaw, a guild also was formed because of a yarn shop and weaving studio. In the early 1970s, Lucinda Jesse began taking weaving lessons from Roz Berlin at her weaving studio in Saginaw's "Old Town"

Wall hanging made by the Niles Handweavers Guild for the Niles Community Library, installed October 15, 1973. (Photo courtesy of the Niles Handweavers Guild.)

area. Jesse's love of weaving grew, and in 1974, she left her job with the city, deciding to open a yarn shop for weavers and knitters called the Flying Shuttle, near Berlin's studio. Shortly after, Berlin and Jesse decided to organize a local guild, the Saginaw Valley Weavers Guild, which was a source for sharing and learning about weaving for twenty years. Although the guild ceased formal meetings in the early 1990s, a few members meet occasionally over a meal or coffee to discuss their projects, and others have joined a Midland or Lansing guild.[10]

Finding a Teacher

In the spring of 1934, the Ashland Folk School at Grant, in the western part of the state, hired Jo Graham to set up a community weaving program. The school was established to revitalize Danish cultural life in the community, including the arts and crafts. Graham, one of the first students at Hartland, remembers her excitement in learning this new craft: "Never one to hold back at the promise of adventure, I was intrigued by the prospect. Besides, in those bleak depression days, economic considerations were not paramount. If I could teach fifty-two children in a one-room school for $40 a month, I could survive a year on maintenance and a travel allowance . . . [At Hartland] I labored with all the myriad details that make up the weaver's stock in trade. At times it seemed more time was spent under the loom than otherwise, readjusting the ropes that held the treadles or correcting all those other weird things that plague a beginner." Despite this, for Graham, weaving "was a new world and a fascinating one."[11] One of her students, Ruth Cross, drove thirty miles from Muskegon to take her first lessons in weaving. Cross became a committed lifelong weaver and founded the Dunes Spinners and Weavers Guild in Muskegon.

The Dunes Spinners and Weavers Guild, no longer in existence, organized in May 1974. In a local 1975 newspaper article, its members credited Ruth Cross as the "inspiration . . . that resulted in the guild."[12] Cross learned to spin and weave at Hartland with Mary Atwater. She also studied there with Harriet Tidball and joined the MLH as a charter member in 1959. Heidi Huntley, Ruth Cross's student (an award-winning spinner, weaver,

Mary Ippel, wearing her hand-woven jacket, helps set up for the annual Woodland Weavers and Spinners sale at Breton Village in East Grand Rapids, October 17, 2001. (Photo by Julia Daniels. Courtesy of the Woodland Weavers and Spinners.)

and tailor of her handwoven garments), recalls Cross saying that when she returned from Hartland in the 1930s, her father, a public prosecutor in Muskegon, made her a loom (he eventually made six) based on a photograph she had taken there. Cross taught students in Muskegon and Detroit, including her father, who was a prolific weaver until his death at age ninety-six. Together, Ruth and her father wove many articles of clothing and furnishings for the home and had an annual sale at the Cross house. Ruth also made bobbin lace and wrote the monograph *Draft Your Own Name and Weave It* (1978) and another entitled *Miniatures* (undated). She lived at home with her parents, but there were never enough hours in the day, it seemed, for weaving.[13]

Guild records indicate that Walter McBride (director of the Grand Rapids Art Museum beginning in 1956), Mary Sayler, and Libby Crawford were instrumental in founding the Woodland Weavers (today Woodland Weavers and Spinners) in Grand Rapids. Sayler, who had moved to Grand Rapids, taught weaving in her home studio; Crawford, from the Detroit area, had a home in Grand Haven. Both Sayler and Crawford were members of Harriet Tidball's Gampers. Sayler was an excellent spinner and weaver who believed in a solid grounding in both crafts; she loved to weave functional textiles and yardage for garments. For her, the art of

Handwoven cotton luncheon tablecloth by Mary Sayler, ca. 1950–60. (Photo by Pearl Yee Wong. Courtesy of the Michigan State University Museum.)

weaving was "the marriage between beautiful textiles and function." She taught and lectured, was twice the president of the MLH (1973–74 and 1981), edited a column for *Shuttle Spindle and Dyepot*, researched the Shuttle-Craft Guild monograph *Fabric Woven from the Records of Thomas Jackson Weavers of Seventeenth and Eighteenth Century in Yorkshire England*, and co-chaired the first HGA convergence. Even as she approached her seventieth year, she was one of the first to embrace computer technology in weaving. Sayler taught classes through the adult education program for the city of Grand Rapids and privately in her home,[14] where as many as eight students would come every Wednesday morning. Students who studied with Sayler for years looked on her classes as a support group for weaving as well as life issues. Today, in Grand Rapids, her student Jayne Schafer, who also studied with Jochen Ditterich, teaches weekly classes in her home, continuing the tradition of mentoring and supporting weavers.

First There Was Fred

In the Kalamazoo region, Fred Wessels of Richland/Highland Park, who worked at the *Kalamazoo Gazette*, is credited with organizing the Kalamazoo Valley Weavers in March 1951. He and Mrs. Richard Bannish took a weaving course offered to the public at Western Michigan College (now Western

Michigan University) in the fall of 1950. Very enthused about the craft, they learned of other interested weavers nearby. Wessels decided to run an article in the *Gazette*, stating that "a movement was afoot to establish a weavers' guild in Kalamazoo." Through this article, "persons interested in the project were asked to attend a meeting in McCracken Hall on the campus of Western Michigan College . . . [and] about forty to forty-five people turned out."[15] Wessels arranged places to meet—in church parlors, in the old Kalamazoo Museum building, and eventually in members' homes. The guild never formally organized, but it remained active, and when the first-year officers' terms expired, the guild decided that "there was no need to select others, nor was there any desire to do so." Wessels, who was held in high esteem by members, both as a weaver and as a good friend, had "naturally gravitated to the post of unofficial general manager, an arrangement that was highly pleasing to everyone."[16] When the MLH was founded in 1959, six members of the Kalamazoo Valley Weavers attended, and Fred Wessels became the state weaving organization's first treasurer.

Wessels was featured in a number of newspaper articles.[17] He enjoyed inventing time-saving devices and working with machinery. Remembering the depression, and with weaving supplies limited in the 1950s, he also practiced frugality. He collected string while working at the *Kalamazoo Gazette*, and upon his retirement, he used the string to make cotton tubing on a Hobby-Knit Machine that he motorized; from this tubing, he wove rag rugs. As weaving materials were hard to come by prior to the 1970s, when he found an inexpensive and large supply of cotton yarns, he bought a goodly amount; so many of his items were woven with a blue-green cotton yarn that it soon became known as "Kalamazoo green."[18] Wessels's enthusiasm and dedication to the craft, as well as his willingness to serve, made him vital to his guild and the new MLH. By the mid-1960s, however, members of the guild were becoming older, and the guild ceased.

Fortunately, at the same time, a new, young, enthusiastic group in Kalamazoo was eager to learn to weave. Many were taking lessons from Ruth Howard, curator of adult education at the Kalamazoo Museum. A large group of twelve or more were eager to learn and to share what they knew. Alice Henwood recalls that she wanted a guild desperately, saying to her friends: "We ought to have a guild like Fred Wessels had. Then we can learn how to weave, teach each other, and maybe we can get some instructors in."[19] Some members of this new group had attended meetings of the Kalamazoo Valley Weavers and helped mentor the new guild. Others went to the MLH to learn about starting a guild. Martha Yeatman was in Ruth Howard's advanced weaving class and, as one group member, Helen Coats, recalls, "was very interested in getting a guild started then," so she "had gone to an MLH meeting and talked to people to see how you go about having a guild organized."[20] Yeatman undoubtedly learned that there were no specific rules for forming guilds in Michigan. Quite often, a group forms because there is a common interest, and it may remain quite informal. Over time, the group may grow in size and wish to become more formal, more organized. Some larger guilds have written constitutions and bylaws that require election of officers and voting on activities and policies of the group.

The new group founded the Weavers Guild of Kalamazoo in 1968, with a sale. It was the jump start for this vibrant group, whose focus and desire was to learn, mentor, and share, with each other and the community. "We taught each other because there was no other resource," Sharon Ford said.[21] Karen Kunze talks of an underlying principle of sharing: "I think that the people who came in and joined as we went along were of the same fiber as the original members. They had the same strength, the same ambition, the same energy, desire to learn, desire to work, willingness. It's all there—you can see that all there today."[22] Especially important, says Elizabeth Clark, was the passing of knowledge: "Except for going to workshops, you didn't really have a chance to learn new techniques. So we were all kind of sponges for that. We would read something or one of us would go to a workshop, and we'd come back and teach the other people. And that was how it worked—each one teach one—the old South African system of passing the knowledge along."[23] These are some among the many strengths of guilds. Brenda Mergen, a charter member, adds, "The guild survives because it's made up of wonderful people that have a real common interest

Anna May teaches a young student how to weave during a demonstration by the Weavers Guild of Kalamazoo. (Photo courtesy of the Weavers Guild of Kalamazoo.)

that's important to them."[24] As the guild began its thirtieth year, charter member Esther James recalled other strengths: "Along the road we have shared the arrival of babies, grandchildren, trips all over the world, work assignments in far off places, kids going to college—then getting jobs, getting married and settling down—and the cycle still goes on. We have shared our homes, our triumphs, and our tragedies and have made lasting friends. We have also mourned together for those who have left us. We have been like a family."[25]

Mentoring

The Midland FiberArts Guild began in 1969, when Bernice Sizemore put an announcement in the *Midland Daily News* that anyone interested in weaving and related arts should meet at her home. Sizemore, who was working with Professor Katherine Ux at Central Michigan University on her BFA with a concentration in weaving, was greatly inspired by her mentor and hoped to start a guild in her hometown.[26] Several women came to the meeting, and together they formed the Weaving and Related Arts Group. Through the years, their programs and workshops focused on handweaving and also other fiber arts. As a result, the guild underwent changes, including its new name. The guild has maintained a close relationship with the Midland Center for the Arts since its opening in 1971. At that time, guild members helped paint and varnish tables and storage cupboards in the new weaving studio, and many were in the first adult weaving class held at the center and led by Bernice Sizemore.[27] Now called the Alden B. Dow Museum of Science and Art, the organization continues its support of fiber in all its forms by encouraging workshops, weaving classes, the Midland Area Weavers Study Group, and fiber exhibits, including *Space Sails: American Banners* (1982, 1986); *Woven by the Griswolds* (1983); *Art to Wear* (1985); *Woven: Four Exhibitions of Woven Textiles*, including JoAnn Bachelder's work: *Levels, Layers, Strata, Positions* (1996); and *Functional Fibers* and *Fascination with Fiber* (2005).

In nearby North Oakland, guild members join together with other guilds for learning experiences, as well as shows and sales. The North Oakland Handweavers Guild (NOHG), begun in 1976 by Trudy Johnson and Pat Parrish informally as a fiber group, reorganized in 1980 to focus on handweaving, with the objective to give all members a networking foundation and the "responsibility to learn together—helping one another."[28] Collaborating with other guilds is very rewarding. In 1984–85, after a year of focusing on the overshot pattern and working on a friendship coverlet, the guild joined with the Black Sheep Weavers and the Genesee Valley Fiber Guild to produce a *Fashioned by Hand* show and sale. In the following two years, the NOHG hosted two triguild meetings with the same guilds, and in 1991–92, the three guilds held a triguild meeting at Waldenwoods, with

Mary Atwater, aged seventy-six, demonstrates for Osma Gallinger, *center*, and Loraine Kessenich, *at left*, while attending the National Conference of American Handweavers in Detroit, August 1954. (Photocopy from the *Detroit Times*, August 17, 1954.)

Madelyn van der Hoogt, the present editor of *Handwoven Magazine*, as guest speaker.

Conferences and Juried Shows

In the early 1950s, two Detroit guilds were very busy. The Michigan Weavers Guild and the Detroit Handweavers Guild (1948, changed to the Detroit Handweavers and Spinners Guild in 1966) hosted a National Conference of American Handweavers. This conference of 125 weavers from across the United States and Canada, featuring prominent speakers, was held at the International Institute in Detroit in August 1954 and at Hartland in 1955.

The Michigan Weavers Guild (MWG), organized in 1947 and known originally as the Southern Michigan Weavers, has had a strong presence in weaving in the Detroit community and carries on an active monthly program of speakers, workshops, and study projects. The Detroit Hand-weavers and Spinners Guild was founded one year later (1948) by Wayne State University weaving teacher Nellie Sargent Johnson. In 1972, the two guilds worked together to help the MLH host the first HGA convergence. During its early years and into the 1960s, the MWG also had developed traveling exhibits to share techniques and information with guilds around the country.

Study groups have been a vital part of guild activities, learning, and growth. The Multi-Harness Study Group, which the MWG began in 1975, became so large that, in 1995, members decided to change its name to Cross Border Weavers (in recognition of its international membership) and to become a separate guild. Over the years, Cross Border Weavers has shared its knowledge of weave structures through programs and demonstrations for the MWG and through exhibits at the MLH conferences. The Cross Border guild studies weave structures for a year or two, and members share samples and discuss techniques. Recent studies include network drafting, rep weave, double weave, unit weave, and corkscrew twill.

Several Michigan weavers are also members of the national organization of Complex Weavers, founded in 1978 by a few individuals at the Midwest Weavers Conference. The Complex Weavers meet in biennial conferences following the HGA convergence. Although it is not a requirement for membership, many of the Complex Weavers work at computerized looms. They develop and share projects in weave structure through long-distance study groups and at conferences. In the 1970s through the 1990s, there was a Complex Weavers study group located in Detroit, but that ceased as an organized group. The current representative of the Complex Weavers to the MLH is Sue Walton. Verda Elliott was a founding member and also the first MLH representative. Information on the Complex Weavers is available at their Web site (http://www.complex-weavers.org).

The Finnish Cultural Association (FCA) of Farmington Hills provides the opportunity for members of the FinnWeavers Fiber Guild to hold sales and shows twice a year—during Springfest and in the fall at the Holiday Bazaar. The FinnWeavers, an active group within FCA, began with the idea of master weaver and spinner Lydia Paris, who wanted to share her knowledge of weaving learned in Finland. Paris spoke with FCA education secretary Eva Koskimaki, and an announcement was made to the membership. In January 1984, the first recorded business meeting was held. While an active member, Paris focused each year on a Finnish project and technique; in later years, other weaving projects were studied. Members include celebrated rag rug weavers Bea Raisanen and Laina Lampi, the latter a founding member. Raisanen was awarded the Michigan Heritage Award in 2002 in recognition of her skill in this craft as well as her dedication in teaching it to others; Lampi has taught many members of her family, including grandchildren, to weave. Both women have won numerous blue ribbons at the

Michigan State Fair, and Lampi has won four best-of-show ribbons. Traditional Finnish rag rug weaving was featured by guild members at the Folk Life Festival in East Lansing in 2000–2001.[29]

Travel and Learn

The guilds that were forming throughout the state provided opportunities for their members to share knowledge about weaving, patterns, and sources for weaving supplies, as well as being a support group of like-minded friends. Kay Holman, founding member of the Blue Pots in Marquette, said members taught each other and learned new techniques and patterns from each other. When they formed, Maybelle Frei suggested the name Blue Pots, based on the Appalachian tradition of indigo dyeing that she had learned about in Berea, Kentucky. The guild decided to borrow the name to continue the tradition of passing skills from one generation to the next and to honor the craft of weaving. Each Appalachian family of weaving women had its own unique shade of indigo blue, and the dyes had highly personalized formulas. They used mordant to set dyes so colors would not fade or run, and, according to Holman, the women used urine for the mordant. Although the Blue Pots borrowed the name, they did not use this method of dyeing.[30]

Limited interactions and connections with other weavers, other than through newsletters or an occasional weaver visiting a guild while vacationing, prompted guilds nationwide to share what they were learning through traveling exhibits. The records of the guilds founded during the 1940s discuss traveling exhibits from other states and those that their members developed. The Michigan Weavers Guild records mention a hat exhibit and a purse exhibit their members shared with other guilds. Guild newsletters give commentaries about traveling exhibits they have displayed at meetings.[31] The fall 1969 issue of *Handweaver and Craftsman* advertised, "The Town and Country Weavers of Michigan have a traveling exhibition of place mats ready to exchange with other guilds." A contact name and address was provided.[32]

Guild members were anxious to learn the newest techniques from prominent weavers and invited lecturers and workshop leaders, such as Dorothea Hulse of Los Angeles, California, who wove the robe used in the movie entitled *The Robe*. Guild records indicate that a number of guilds across Michigan hosted Hulse during the mid- to later 1950s, including the Niles Handweavers Guild at Fernwood, the Greater Lansing Weavers Guild, and guilds in the Detroit area. A booklet of instructions for a workshop held in Detroit on April 22–26, 1956, states that guild members participating in the workshop came from "Ann Arbor, Mich[igan,] and the guild there, Town and Country Handweavers of Michigan, the Detroit Handweaving Guild, and the Michigan Weavers Guild." There were also "several weavers from Ontario, Canada, from the Windsor area as well as a goodly number who made the trip back and forth from Leamington." Everyone loved Mrs. Hulse's workshops, due to her graciousness and the "outstanding quantity and variety of textiles [she brought], designed and woven by high ranking leaders in the field of handweaving."[33]

Handspinning Revival Creates New Opportunities

During the 1970s, many guilds were forming as a result of the craft revival. The Michigan Handspinners Guild (MHG), which began meeting in 1972, formally organized in 1974. At the time, the craft of spinning was almost a lost skill, and the MHG was the only active Michigan guild devoted totally to the art of spinning. The guild's constitution states that the guild is dedicated to "the enjoyment of handspinning through the sharing of spinning experiences and information and to stimulate public appreciation of handspinning." Members grew in knowledge and experience, and by 1995–96, the group had grown to a peak of seventy-two members, drawing spinners from Lapeer, Saint Clair, the Lansing area, and New Boston. As handspinning grew in popularity, smaller groups split off to start on their own. The Woolgatherers, organized by Carol Isleib of East Lansing, was such a group. In the mid-1970s, Isleib advertised in the *Lansing State Journal* about starting a spinning group. The meeting was held in the community room of the East Lansing Public Library, where the guild met each month thereafter. One attendee who mistakenly thought she was attending a meeting of the League of Women Voters stayed on and eventually held a guild board position and learned to spin. Another guild, Delta Weavers, beginning with seven members, also organized in the mid-1970s (1977), based on its strong interest in fiber and fleece.

Because of the resurgence of interest in handspinning and the "very difficult task of finding suitable fibers to spin," the MHG developed a series of wool sales and conferences called "Spinaround." Its early beginnings started with sales of wool fleece (supplied by a local farmer) in Carol Isleib's garage in East Lansing, held by her guild, the Woolgatherers. When the sales became too large for her garage, Isleib, also a member of the MHG, brought the idea of the sale to the larger guild, and the members liked it. Through the energy of member Doris Loftis and other guild members, the MHG held its first sale in Haslett, Michigan, on April 1, 1978.[34] Spinaround became an annual event that brought together handspinners, wool sellers, and new spinners. By 1982, it had become an important conference for the whole Great Lakes area and nearby Canada and was held biennially. The largest conference, held at Macomb County Community College in 1998, attracted over three hundred people. As Spinaround grew, national teachers were invited to further enhance the educational component of the conference. They stayed on to work with guild members, increasing their knowledge.[35] After its largest conference, in 1998, the MHG discontinued Spin-around, as members decided that the conference involved a tremendous amount of work and was too great a commitment for the guild to continue at the time. To date, Spinaround has not been restarted.

Other organizations with interest in natural fibers sprang up around the state. The Michigan Fiber Festival (MFF) in Allegan, which began in 1997, has grown tremendously in the last few years, to become one of the largest such festivals in the nation. It attracts a large attendance over a five-day period, with many instructors and vendors from around the country and Michigan. The MFF provides a yearly forum for teaching and for exhibiting fiber animals, products, and knowledge. It advances fiber arts within the state and encourages youth involvement in the fiber industry and arts. It also draws a wide range of teachers and fiber artists, such as "the Felt Lady," Suzanne Pufpaff of Nashville. It offers weaving by such Michigan instructors as Ann Neimi of Kessenich Looms, who has taught each year. Susan Halvorson has taught chenille weaving; Andrea Mielke, the inkle loom; and Jill Turner, beginning tapestry. Millie Danielson of Ann Arbor and Jochen Ditterich of Grand Rapids have also been instructors.

In 1980, prior to the formation of the MFF, the Spinner's Flock formally organized as a guild, with five members. The group is located in the Chelsea region and draws membership from across southern Michigan, northern Ohio, and Indiana. As stated in the guild's history, "the group's members are committed to improving and teaching the craft of handspinning and to spreading the good news everywhere of the superior quality of Wonderful Michigan Wool for all kinds of clothing and crafts." During its twenty-five years as a guild, membership has grown to 161, with well over one hundred spinners attending monthly meetings at Beach Middle School in Chelsea. As skills, confidence, and membership increased, the guild decided, in 1984, to hold a Fleece Fair to market their products. Members could sell fleeces, rovings, handspun yarns, skins, and other fibers, as well as spinning equipment and books, knitted and woven garments, and accessories—with the emphasis on Michigan-grown fibers and their products. For the first several years, the Fleece Fair was held in member Nancy Burkhalter's barn. When space became tight and the weather a concern, the sale moved to Matthaei Botanical Gardens. The guild presently holds two sales each year—the Holiday Sale on the Saturday following Thanksgiving and the Winter Fleece Fair on the third Saturday of February (held at Beach Middle School). They are the largest sales in the state after the MFF.[36]

Connecting with the Community

Informal weaving groups are vitally important—sharing information, passing on knowledge, and keeping the craft and art alive. Just as the Kalamazoo

Valley Weavers met in the early 1950s for these purposes, a few groups of weavers and fiber artists meet in downtown Detroit today. Former students from the College for Creative Studies still meet regularly as a group, according to Marcia McDonald. They have taken classes with Mollie Fletcher either in the undergraduate program or in the extension course she offers on Saturdays or in the evenings. The group is comprised of members from different ethnic cultures who enjoy coming together to support each other in their fiber work, according to McDonald, an African American and director of admissions at Wayne State University's law school. McDonald took Fletcher's extension course, but her full-time position does not allow much time for organizations. This group inspires her to continue to explore new ideas, such as differential shrinkage using a new material called *jump*, a rayon-silk blend.[37]

One of the most recently formed groups in Michigan is the Detroit Weavers Group, organized in 2004. Twenty Detroit African American weavers have been identified as potential members. Some of them studied weaving at Wayne State University, Cranbrook Academy of Art, the College for Creative Studies, or the Birmingham Bloomfield Art Center (BBAC). Janet Jones Diones, who has a loom in her Source Booksellers store at the Spiral Staircase building in Detroit, has brought several of these weavers together. They are hoping to find a place where they can share looms and studio space. The group is open to people who identify with Detroit, in contrast to most of the existing weaving guilds that are located in the suburbs. Jones retired from forty years of teaching in the Detroit public school system and was given a loom. She promptly looked for a place to take classes and chose Sue Walton's class at the BBAC. Jones says that when she sits at the loom, she feels connected not only to her African American heritage but also to the larger, international world of weavers. "This is a luxury, a creative opportunity for adults—much better than sitting and watching TV," she says. She grew up around quilting, but weaving is her passion.[38]

Connections between groups of fiber artists and the local community take many forms. In Toledo, for example, the Toledo Area Weavers Guild (a member guild in the MLH), organized in 1947, has met at the Toledo Botanical Garden (TBG) since 1982. The guild, in turn, has become a vital part of the TBG and the wider community, presenting lectures and classes in weaving and fiber arts. Each year, as part of its current commitment to the TBG, the guild conducts two "Grow Ed" public outreach programs—such as weaving workshops—which have been very successful.

The Jackson Handweavers Guild meets at the Ella Sharp Museum and, as an active member of the museum, commits its members' time and energy by hosting receptions and demonstrating for the public. The Mill Race Weavers Guild holds its meetings in a historic weaver's cottage in the Mill Race Historic Village in Northville. The guild's commitment to the com-

The Toledo Area Weavers Guild, June 1954. (Photo courtesy of the Toledo Area Weavers Guild.)

munity and the Northville Historic Society for the use of this free meeting place was "to restore and maintain the cottage as well as educate the community in all aspects of fiber work through teaching, demonstrations, shows, and sales." Over a three-year period, the guild restored the cottage and wove all the furnishings in period style, which required a substantial amount of research and weaving. Since that time, they continue to demonstrate weaving, provide minilectures, and host visitors on Sunday afternoons in the summer.[39] The Northeast Michigan Weavers Guild, which evolved out of SWIFT (Sunrise Weaving and Fiber Techniques), a study group of members from the Sunrise Spinning Guild, is a relatively new guild (established in 1998) that has a wide reach—its seven members come from six counties in northeastern Michigan. The focus of the guild is on teaching and learning and on sharing the members' love of handweaving with their communities. Demonstrations at community events and programs for schoolchildren have been important parts of this outreach. The guild meets at the Jesse Besser Museum in Alpena, and members are involved in a variety of educational programs and exhibits there—participating in the museum's Fall Harvest Day; bringing the John Landes exhibit to the museum in 1998; planning, implementing, and hanging a fiber exhibit, *The Common Thread*, in 1999; and bringing *Fascination with Fiber* in 2005.

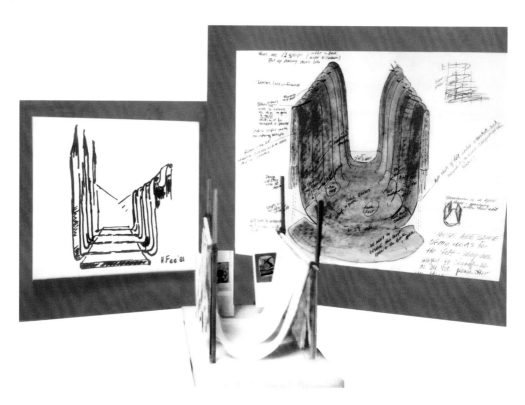

The original sketch and mock-up for the *Fiber Space Shuttle*, an experiential installation designed and completed by the Mill Race Weavers Guild for a conference of the Michigan League of Handweavers, 1981. (Photo courtesy of the Mill Race Weavers Guild.)

Work and Share

In this spirit of working, sharing, and learning together, guild members today, as in the past, are motivated and renewed and form deeper friendships with other members through guild activities. It is documented that when the Livingston County Weavers Guild formed in May 1937, "the guild offered cooperation, sharing, keeping samples and drafts, and renting looms for 24 cents a week."[40] In 1980, the Mill Race Weavers Guild of Northville decided to tackle something they had never envisioned doing before—creating an environmental structure that would involve every member and months of intensive planning and work. Inspired by the theme for the 1981 MLH conference, "New Directions in Fiber Structure," the guild rose to the challenge, making the *Fiber Space Shuttle*. Members interpreted the theme as "any 'new direction' in fibers . . . rooted in an old tradition and serving a contemporary idea." Their new direction was a sculptural form to soften the 1980s architecture of "cold" concrete and metals. The fiber structure created an environment suggesting a modern dwelling space, which

Johanna Stevens and Kathy Zasuwa hang the dyed and washed skeins for drying for the *Fiber Space Shuttle* project, 1981. (Photo courtesy of the Mill Race Weavers Guild.)

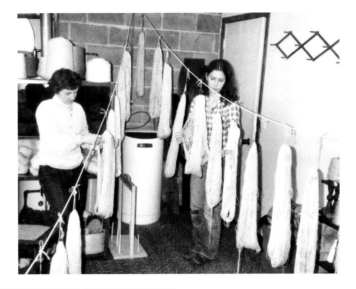

Kathy Zasuwa and Dale Greiner stand beside the *Fiber Space Shuttle*, 1981. (Photo courtesy of the Mill Race Weavers Guild.)

was expanded to involve a visual, tactile, and sensory feast. A design was sketched, samples were made, and yarns were wound, dyed, felted, woven, and assembled. The structure was a huge success at the conference and later traveled to Grand Rapids as an exhibit. Through their working together, members felt the reward of learning something about themselves—their capabilities, aspirations, and souls—and, most of all, they felt "so glad to be weavers."[41]

During 1988–89, members of the Greater Lansing Weavers Guild study group also learned about their capacities for growth and the rewards of working together as a group. As soon as the group learned of that year's MLH conference theme, "Connections," members challenged each other to design and weave a guild exhibit to display at the conference the following summer. *Just Connect*, an innovative and art-oriented exhibit, was different from any project the group had tackled before. After months of studying and experimenting with the Theo Moorman technique and struggling with various ideas for a cohesive statement, one member made a suggestion that finally gelled the concept for the entire group—a connecting line of red to be woven across each neutral-shaded wall hanging at whatever height the weaver wished. When the individual pieces were suspended in a semicircle, the powerful red line tied all the weavings together to make a bold statement. Members learned about their abilities in designing their individual pieces and their part in a group project and garnered the satisfaction of working through a project together to accomplish a desired result. The guild received first place for its efforts.

Community outreach and working with members of the community committed weavers and guilds in the early years and continues today. Weaving was an important handicraft for rehabilitative and therapy purposes in World Wars I and II. Both Mary Atwater and Harriet Tidball were occupational therapists. Atwater stated in her classic weaving book *Byways in Hand-Weaving* (1954): "It is not by chance that handicrafts are used more than any other type of occupation for the purpose. Psychologists tell us that our closest sensations of reality come through the sense of touch."[42] The records of the Greater Lansing Weavers Guild and an article in *Handweaver and Craftsman* reflect that in the mid-1950s, members sold handwoven items in their first project—called "Weaverama"—to raise funds for various purposes, including the purchase of a loom for therapy. The loom was donated to the Ingham County Curative Workshop, "where scores of partially paralyzed persons of all ages are helped to retrain damaged muscles resulting from many causes."[43] Guild members in 1956 began another service project—helping warp looms at the Michigan School for the Blind in Lansing. Through the years, guilds have also served the community by working with children in local schools and demonstrating spinning and weaving at local community, art, and street fairs and at the Michigan State Fair in Detroit.

Two members of the Ann Arbor Fiberarts Guild, Georgia Gleason and Marion Marzolf, began to demonstrate and teach weaving at the University of Michigan Cancer Center in 2002 to help patients pass the time while waiting for appointments. The project expanded when member Bettie Bahen used the weaving to make hats for the patients and when Phyllis Thompson donated warps she prepared.[44]

Since its founding in 1956, the Ann Arbor guild has been involved in many community activities. Its nineteen charter members, with such leaders as Joyce Jones, prominent in Ann Arbor and Michigan weaving circles, were active in helping to establish the Ann Arbor Street Art Fair. Jones was its registrar for fifteen years, until her death in 1980. The guild's booth, which draws many visitors during this large summer fair, has been a part of the State Street Area Art Fair since the 1960s. Today, the guild is a group of

Left: Bettie Bahen modeling one of the hats she designed and created for patients from a warp woven at the University of Michigan Cancer Center, 2002. (Photo by Marion T. Marzolf. Courtesy of the Ann Arbor Fiberarts Guild.)

Right: A warp woven by Georgia Gleason, Marion Marzolf, and cancer patients during a University of Michigan Cancer Center project, 2002. (Photo by Marion T. Marzolf. Courtesy of the Ann Arbor Fiberarts Guild.)

140 fiber artists who enjoy meeting to exchange ideas. Comments in a recent *Ann Arbor News* article reflect members' enthusiasm and involvement in their guild. Millie Danielson said, "Folks who are immersed in the fiber world tend to be fun and spirited." Talking of guild activities and sharing time, Susan Anderson said: "One of the things we provide is the chance for someone who has never shown anything of theirs before to show it to us . . . It gives them a sense of self worth but also helps them to accept suggestions."[45]

The booth of the Ann Arbor Fiberarts Guild at the Ann Arbor State Street Area Art Fair, 1992. (Photo by Nancy Burkhalter. Courtesy of the Ann Arbor Fiberarts Guild.)

Guild Programs and Workshops

Guild programs and workshops reflect broad topics of interest. For example, in 1982, the Dunes Spinners and Weavers Guild invited Willem Clous from Grand Rapids to present a program on *passement* (ornamental braid) weaving. As part of the program, he brought along his collection of family-owned weaving diaries that were nearly two hundred years old to share with guild members.[46] In 1985, the Greater Lansing Weavers Guild invited Walter Adams from Michigan State University to talk about the weaving co-operative that he and his mother had established in Central America. Millie Danielson, in the 1990s, presented a program on tapestries in France from her travels there; in 2003, Martha Brownscombe, after a recent trip to Peru, displayed handwoven garments and textiles and handspun yarns during her presentation about cooperatives and weaving shops in that region of South America. Programs are also interactive: Lakeshore Fiber Arts Guild members, for example, recently worked in miniature for the Beaded Prayers Project, painted and printed paste papers for book covers, pounded leaves into fabric for Cherokee leaf printing, folded origami boxes, and transferred family photos to fabric, during their program meetings. Other groups have woven tapes and made tassels and *kumihimo* braids. In the early 1990s, the North Oakland Handweavers Guild joined the Black Sheep Weavers for a workshop called "Bevy of Belts." As a part of the project, members were to provide a record sheet, draft, and sample for each guild member at the end of the year. They decided to submit samples for Carol Strickler's *A Weaver's Book of 8-Shaft Patterns from the Friends of Handwoven* (1991), which resulted in eight of the guild members being published.[47]

Guild programs and workshops today have expanded to include traditional weave structures and new fiber-art techniques, surface design techniques, computer-related topics, clothing construction, dyeing techniques, and spinning. Guilds also make innovative use of their local natural environments in the pursuit of fiber interests. The Yarnwinders Fiber Guild in Marquette, located on Lake Superior and other nearby lakes, used lake

Watching the pots at an outdoor dye workshop, 1973. *In the foreground, from left:* Barbara Forsberg, Sarah Beyer, Mary Miller, and Anita Meyland. (Photo courtesy of the Yarnwinders Fiber Guild.)

Yarnwinders Fiber Guild members Mary Miller, *left*, and Vivian Glass at a gravel pit during a dye workshop, 1981. (Photo courtesy of the Yarnwinders Fiber Guild.)

water to wash their hats, for example, during a 1977 workshop on felting. Guild members worked outdoors—and even at a gravel pit—during dye workshops on different occasions. Lakes, woods, gardens, backyards, decks, and porches have served as inspiring and useful places to experiment and work. Guilds are quick to pick up on new research at their nearby art schools. Recently, the Ann Arbor Fiberarts Guild hosted Rowland Ricketts, a weaving student at Cranbrook. In 1996–97, Ricketts was an apprentice in Japan, studying the production of traditional indigo dye, its natural fermentation, and shibori. Ricketts plans to set up a farm in the United States to produce indigo dye and to teach Americans how to use it. His wife, Chinami, a native of Japan, is also a weaver and shibori artist.[48] Workshop programs planned by guilds in 2005 ranged from the traditional to new techniques and included Bonnie Inouye's "The Big Twill," JoAnn Bachelder's "Three-Shaft Weaving," Suzanne Halverson's "Weaving with Chenille," Gisela Bosch's "Shadow Weave Workshop," Kathy Zasuwa's "Beyond Basics in Moorman," Linda Henrickson's "Ply-Split Braiding," and Kay Faulkner's "Loom-Controlled Shibori."

Heirlooms

As in the past, some Michigan weavers today are also creating family heirlooms through the textiles they weave; others are carrying on ethnic and

Weaver Kala Exworthy washes her hat (in process) in Lake Independence at a guild felting workshop, 1997. (Photo by Patty Beyer. Courtesy of the Yarnwinders Fiber Guild.)

cultural traditions. Pat Chipman, for example, wove an MLH prize-winning wool child's coat in 1981 that has been used by seven children in her family. As she was planning her wedding in 1991, Karen East decided to make her own dress. The result was a beautifully woven silk wedding dress in a huck lace pattern, embellished with beads. Esther James, who has eighteen grandchildren, decided to weave yardage of silk and cotton for a christening gown and hat for her great-grandchildren, each of whose names she intends will be embroidered on the hem of the dress. James completed the heirloom set with the help of her good friend Sharon Ford, who did the designing and sewing. Carol Isleib, teacher of spinning and weaving, has won awards for her work in double-weave pickup and enjoys designing and weaving bookmarks, among other items. Isleib made her first bookmark for her father. Her love of making bookmarks each year resulted in the publication of two articles about them in *Handwoven Magazine*.

Guilds continue to introduce new work and ideas while promoting high standards of craftsmanship. Members form lifelong friendships and bonds of sharing knowledge and serving the community. The guilds have the funds and numbers to offer study groups, guest lectures, workshops, newsletters, exhibits, libraries, and sales opportunities for their members. Untold hours of volunteer time and energy keep these organizations vital. Accomplished weavers and novices are welcomed and nurtured and folded into guild activities. In many parts of the state, the guilds are the primary centers of knowledge and information about the fiber arts, the carriers of tradition and the introducers of the new. Jean Brudzinski of the Michigan Weavers Guild emphasized: "I can't stress too much about friendships that you can make working with people who have a common interest. It's not that people weave the same or make the same sorts of things. It's just the idea of making something that you think of, that comes from your own thoughts, and your own hands—and being with people who do the same thing."[49]

FASCINATION WITH FIBER

SIX

Art Centers, Museums, and Shops

Such organizations as fiber and yarn shops, weaving shops, art centers, and museums have been and continue to be invaluable in keeping craft alive and well in Michigan. They have been a source for the purchase of supplies and a place to go for weaving instruction and, for some, encouragement in a new craft. They also provide the means for sales opportunities and exhibitions of fiber work and are a source of award prizes in juried competitions.

Weaving in Grand Rapids

In Grand Rapids, weaving instruction seems to have first been organized in 1948 by the Grand Rapids Art Gallery (later the Grand Rapids Art Museum), until 1981, when it was no longer taught there.[1] In the meantime, The Weaver's Shop opened in the 1970s at Rockford, fifteen miles north, and the Threadbender Yarn Shop—where area weavers could find supplies and instruction—set up business in 1984 in Wyoming. Betty Hagberg, whose first husband, Richard Yonkers, was the director of the Grand Rapids Art Gallery from 1945 through 1954, convinced Betty to teach classes in the gallery's basement: "[There] was an old black two-harness loom—an old wooden loom with a very rusty reed. I was not remotely interested in that loom. I thought it should be moved out of there because it was taking up space. But my husband . . . said, 'Well there's a loom here. Why don't we begin with that?' And I said, 'Well, who knows how to weave?' And he said, 'I'll go to Cranbrook and learn how to weave. And I'll come back and teach you what I know, and you can teach weaving. We'll get some more looms.' . . . so Richard went off to Cranbrook and learned how to weave. And he wove a sampler, a wonderful sampler, in which each assignment was probably twelve inches long, in many techniques, none of them pattern weaving. This was contemporary weaving, with different threads and textures and design . . . [and] he came back and I had a weaving studio. I ended up with thirteen looms."

Thus, Hagberg began teaching the museum's class, which offered college credit through the University of Michigan Extension Program beginning in 1954. Hagberg recalls: "I knew very little about weaving . . . and I would have faltered miserably, except for the fact that this was right after the war when many displaced persons came from abroad. And because Grand Rapids was a Dutch community, a lot of Dutch people came. And one evening after the class had just started, a man appeared and asked if he could join the weaving class. This was Bob Clous [Willem Clous]. He was a marvelous weaver. He had a career in the Netherlands being a trouble-shooter for the looms of Holland. He went from workshop to workshop repairing looms, warping looms, et cetera. He was a fine weaver himself . . . [but] he never got a chance to weave on the looms. He became my assistant, and we had large weaving classes. We would put on a 50 yard warp. We had students who did upholsteries and draperies. We had a woman who had a regular warehouse full of silk stockings of all colors, and she wanted a 9 by 12 rug. She proceeded to weave and sew her sections together until she had a 9 by 12 rug. Another student . . . wanted to do neckties. I spent most of my time on my stomach underneath the looms, tying them up and trying to adjust the tensions for the students."[2] During the years when Hagberg was busy with weaving and students, her husband studied with Anni and Josef Albers at Black Mountain College in North Carolina and brought back new ideas.

In 1956, Walter McBride became the director of the Grand Rapids Art Gallery (retiring in 1970). During his tenure, the gallery changed its name to the Grand Rapids Art Museum. McBride, a former art teacher and watercolorist, became a weaver after a study tour of Sweden. "I love to spin and weave," he commented at age ninety-six, adding, "You have to concentrate and your worries go out the door." He and his wife, Lois, a teacher and fiber artist who excelled in needlework and embroidery, were very supportive of exhibits of fiber art at the Grand Rapids Art Museum. McBride curated a number of particularly noteworthy exhibits. The 1970s exhibit—a national show called *The Magic of Fibers*—was in tune with the times. It featured fifty artists and 145 works, including many by Grand Rapids fiber artists.[3] At the time of America's bicentennial in 1976, McBride curated another significant exhibit, *Our Heritage in Weaving 76*, which looked back to the country's early handwovens as exemplified primarily in coverlets. The exhibit also included modern-day handwoven pieces by weavers in Michigan guilds who reinterpreted the early American textiles and patterns. Weaving was an important part of the program of arts and crafts classes offered at the art museum.

During the 1960s, Cranbrook graduate Robert Sailors taught weaving in Grand Rapids at the gallery/museum, after he moved his studio from Bitely to Belmont. He attracted weavers from a wide radius.[4] Jochen Ditterich, who had learned to weave in Finland, remembers seeing "a little ad" about the class. Ditterich's wife was a University of Michigan graduate and received announcements about their extension courses. Ditterich recalls: "There was one listed for weaving at the Grand Rapids Art Gallery. I said to my wife, 'I really would like to go back and do that.' Bob Sailors was the teacher at the time. I went in there and started weaving and had a ball. I stayed three years."[5] Weavers from Kalamazoo recall their related experiences. Esther James said: "I remember Bob Sailors coming to talk to us. And he gave workshops at KIA [the Kalamazoo Institute of Arts], too. He would bring these beautiful yarns and explain what they were, like loop mohair and chenille and rayon and all these beautiful things. And he would put them all in the warps. He did a lot of the blinds for Big Boy [restaurants] at one time I believe—and put a lot of these fancy yarns in those."[6] Helen Coats remembered the excitement about Sailors's classes: "Joyce Lemin and Renata Taylor and Elizabeth Clark all worked at Upjohn [in Kalamazoo]. They would get off work and drive up [together] to Grand Rapids for his class and then they would drive back! . . . They learned a lot."[7]

Jochen Ditterich made weaving his full-time career when he opened The Weaver's Shop and Yarn Company in Rockford, north of Grand Rapids, on Memorial Day in 1975. The shop became another vital center for weavers and fiber artists. Housed in a large two-story building on the north side

The Weaver's Shop and Yarn Company, Rockford, Michigan, Christmas 1988. (Photo courtesy of Jochen and Nancy Ditterich.)

of the town square, it provided a much-needed place for those wanting to learn to weave, to purchase supplies and equipment (including looms), and to sell their handwoven items. Its store windows and front room displayed handwoven items, and the back room had ceiling-high shelves full of colorful yarns and a large variety of weaving, spinning, and knitting gadgets. The sounds of classical music floated through the rooms from the weaving studio on the second floor. A climb up the wooden stairs took one to the airy studio, full of floor looms (about twenty-four LeClerc and Glimåkra looms, primarily). Ditterich gave weaving lessons on Tuesday and Thursday evenings on a monthly basis. Special weeklong workshops were led by such noted weavers as Albertje Koopman, formerly of the Netherlands, and Peter Collingwood of England.[8]

The Norwood Loom of Baldwin

Baldwin, east of Ludington, where Mary Sayler came to learn weaving, had been a weaving center since 1950 when Robert and Gladys Rogers Brophil opened the Warp and Weft Shop. Robert Brophil manufactured looms in one room; in another room, his wife, Gladys, a designer and weaver, displayed and sold textiles from around the country and even as far away as Australia. The shop also carried products made by amateur weavers and craftspeople and by handicapped and elderly persons who were supplementing retirement incomes from their handiwork. Gladys Brophil was an occupational therapist who worked with handicapped persons in the area to develop their talents. Soon after the Brophils started their manufacturing business, Wallace McGarr joined them to build the handsome cherry Norwood looms.[9] He was a woodworker and, within a short time, bought the loom business and set about improving the look and quality of the looms. His wife, Melvina, joined him in the business. She learned to weave at Hartland and from other weavers because their customers needed help. Weaving became her lifetime interest, and the couple expanded the shop to include works of one hundred regional craftspeople. Customers came from all over the state and beyond to buy a loom and take classes.[10]

When McGarr retired in 1974, Ted and Nancy Johnson bought the Norwood loom business, and their son, Dave, joined the company. They began producing the Cranbrook loom in 1980, obtaining the rights from Heritage Woodcrafts, which had only owned them a few years. The two popular looms were produced in Baldwin for some time, but Dave Johnson was ready for a change by the mid-1990s. Production of the Norwood looms was sold to the Webs Company of Massachusetts, and they are currently produced in partnership with Toika of Finland. The Cranbrook production went to Schacht Spindle Company of Colorado.[11] That left Michigan with only

Wallace and Melvina McGarr of Norwood Loom Company demonstrate weaving during a parade in Baldwin, Michigan, ca. 1959. (Photo courtesy of McGarr Family History.)

one loom in production, that of the Kessenich Loom Company, originating in Wisconsin in 1945, but owned since 1993 by Bruce and Ann Niemi of Allegan, Michigan.

Guilds and Weaving Centers Connect

In Kalamazoo, weaving was taught by Ruth Howard at the Kalamazoo Museum, located on the second floor of the public library. Howard taught many of the founding members of the Weavers Guild of Kalamazoo; she was well loved as a teacher and mentor. Her student Esther James calls her "the matriarch of weaving in Kalamazoo" and recalls: "She was teacher to many of us. She arranged for the meetings at the Museum. She knew more than any of us and we needed her. Ruth didn't drive, but a group of us always saw to it that she was picked up and delivered to the meetings and returned home when it was over. After she retired and moved to Ionia, she continued to come to our meetings, taking the bus to Kalamazoo, staying with one of us over night . . . and returning home the next day. She kept busy supervising the building of her *Loomy Bin* at her home where she taught weaving."[12] Elizabeth Clark, another founding member of the Weavers Guild of Kalamazoo, had opened the Weaver's Shed, a downtown shop for yarn and weaving supplies, and was giving lessons—but with limited hours, as she worked full-time at Upjohn. Martha Yeatman, a guild member, became the weaving instructor at Saginaw Valley State College in the 1970s and helped start the weaving program at the Kalamazoo Institute of

Arts (KIA) in 1971. The program was taught by Barbara DePeaux until 1978.[13] Several other teachers have taught weaving classes at the KIA, including Helmi Moulton and Eve Reid, both from the art department at Western Michigan University. Currently, the weaving classes at KIA are taught by Gretchen Huggett.

In Midland, Professor Katherine Ux helped Bernice Sizemore start the Midland Arts Council's weaving program at the Midland Center for the Arts. It opened on October 6, 1971, offering thirty-two hours of lessons for thirty-five dollars. Sizemore was very interested in the planning and opening of the new center and mentioned to her friend Helen James, who was on the Midland Art Association's committee, one of the art committees interested in forming a Midland Center for the Arts, that "it would be awfully nice if we had a weaving studio and classes." James brought the idea to the members of her committee, who agreed. Professor Ux was consulted for purchasing looms and supplies. "When they asked her whom she would recommend to teach the classes, bless her heart, she chose me," Sizemore said.[14] Sizemore's classes were usually full. In addition to instruction, weaving workshops were given throughout the years by such well-known authorities as Peter Collingwood and Budd Stalnaker and by Michigan artist-weavers Mollie Fletcher, Libby Crawford, and Verda Elliott, to name a few. Katherine Ux occasionally gave design workshops. Sizemore also arranged spinning workshops at the Unitarian Universalist Church in Midland. Finnish spinner Vieno Mikkola gave a program on the spinning of yarn, with the aid of Mrs. Frances Itter, who "acted as interpreter."[15] In July 2000, Sizemore compiled scrapbooks of the adult weaving classes and their activities, documenting the fiber art created there during the years of 1971–87. Sizemore, who has received many commissions for her artwork, creates unique wall hangings that are woven or rich in surface design techniques, such as appliqué and needlework—following the lead of her mentor, Katherine Ux. Sizemore has created personal garments for herself and others. When she attended the first conference of the Handweavers Guild of America in 1972 at Detroit as a charter member, she was garbed in a floor-length evening gown and matching stole that she had designed and woven. After her retirement in 1987, the adult weaving program at the Midland Arts Council (now the Alden B. Dow Museum of Science and Art) continued under her student JoAnn Bachelder of Bay City.

Bachelder remembers her first lessons with Sizemore: "We experimentated with different kinds of yarns, and we painted the warp . . . and made rya knots. We did all the weaver control things we were encouraged to try." Bachelder continued to learn, adding more to her knowledge of weaving from workshops through the MLH. Bachelder taught the adult weaving program until 2002, when she retired to devote more time to her craft at her weaving studio, Rivertown Textiles in Bay City. Today, Susan Dudzik, also a student of Katherine Ux, is the current weaving instructor at

Midland and continues the weaving heritage there. Teacher-student mentoring flowed from Katherine Ux to her students, enriching the communities of Mount Pleasant, Midland, and Bay City with artist-weavers who taught.

In nearby Flint, weaving was offered at the Flint Institute of Arts beginning in 1937 by Swedish-born Lillian Holm, who came from the Kingswood School at Cranbrook one day a week for many years.[16] She taught Swedish weaving techniques to students who wove linens, tapestries, and wool yardage, primarily.[17] Later, Marie Sayles, Christine Mair, Bessie Revere, Rita Kent, Libby Keenon, and Leslie Heinstadt taught the weaving classes. The program is presently taught by Alice Foster-Stocum, the great niece of Christine Mair. She has supplemented the ten-week program with classes in tapestry, dyeing, and spinning. Foster-Stocum remembers that her great aunt was a member of the MLH and a wonderful teacher: "She would allow you to discover your own mistakes rather than pointing it out immediately." Mair could spot mistakes very readily, and in her generation, weavers wove a lot of yardage for clothing. Foster-Stocum recalls her great aunt standing behind her as she wove and saying nothing about a mistake. Then, after about six inches or so of weaving, when Foster-Stocum still had not noticed the mistake, Mair pointed it out and said: "See that little mistake there? On a jacket, it might be right between the shoulders and look like a bull's eye."[18]

Weaving is also regularly taught today at the Birmingham Bloomfield Hills Art Center by Sue Walton, an artist-weaver whose specialty is clothing. During the early 1960s, when Barbara Wittenberg, who later studied at Cranbrook, first learned to weave, the center was known as Bloomfield Art Association (BAA). It was an ideal place for Cranbrook teachers and graduates to teach weaving. Eleen Auvil of Romeo, Michigan, was Wittenberg's instructor. She had received her MFA in weaving from Cranbrook in 1961, and by the fall of 1968, she was head of the weaving program at Wayne State University. Auvil's early textiles for interiors—pillows and matching mohair throws—were very much in demand in specialty shops and better retail department stores across the country. In 1964, her work expanded into a variety of interiors (from window screens to bedspreads), and she won the International Design Award from the American Institute of Interior Designers.[19] Wittenberg recalls Auvil's marvelous ability to combine colors. When Auvil left, Robert Kidd, head of Cranbrook's fiber department from 1968 through 1970, taught at BAA. Wittenberg said that the time during which she studied there with Kidd was "when I really started to weave."[20] Wittenberg continued under Kidd's and Gerhardt Knodel's direction at Cranbrook from 1969 to 1971 to earn her MFA. While at Cranbrook, she wove only wall pieces, but after graduation, Wittenberg began making handwoven garments and giving her own workshops. Before learning to weave, she began sewing as a child, and garment making came easily to her. Wittenberg was soon leading workshops in clothing construction, the making of T-shaped bog jackets and kachina dolls (to teach about kente cloth[21] and double weave, respectively), overshot, and dyeing. As a workshop instructor, it was important to her to complete a project: "You have to teach something beyond [weaving only samples] . . . It has to go beyond that to be satisfying." During the 1970s and early 1980s, Wittenberg traveled and taught frequently across the country and was keynote speaker for conferences in the Midwest and the Northwest.[22]

Robert Kidd worked on his MFA at Cranbrook with Marianne Strengell, who Kidd says was a wonderful teacher: "You really learned fiber from the roots up." He was asked to teach at Cranbrook and headed the fiber program from 1968 to 1970, but he left to start his own business—Robert L. Kidd Associates, a studio in Bloomfield Hills, with a staff of weavers that did commission work for about fifteen years. Kidd was known for his large custom-designed wall hangings, bedspreads, and flossa (short pile) work—for interiors and industry. He met Ray Fleming, who headed the Kingswood School at Cranbrook, and together they decided to open a gallery to sell their own work. In 1975, the gallery opened in Birmingham, Michigan. The Robert L. Kidd Gallery has developed to be one of the largest in the state. "One of the problems with running a weaving studio is the equipment and the big supply of fibers you need," Kidd says. It was sometimes overwhelming. Currently, Kidd is devoting time to developing new prototype yarns for the mills, as many of the good yarn sources for weavers no longer exist. In a 1972 article, he was quoted as saying, "Weaving is more than an occupation—it is a way of life." He still believes it.[23]

Following Kidd as instructors at BAA were Urban Jupena in the early 1970s, Barbara Wittenberg, and Verda Elliott, who taught Sue Walton in 1980. Margaret Windeknecht followed Elliott as instructor, and Germaine Smith taught from 1983 until her retirement in 1998. Walton received her BS in art education at the Miami University in Ohio and continued the program after Smith. She currently teaches students in all levels of instruction. Term classes are typically filled with three to seven students, many of whom have been with Walton since 1998.[24]

Village Looms Not Just for Display

In the Detroit area, the Greenfield Village weaving program started many weavers on their path. Bessie C. Lowry, who became serious about weaving when she studied at Greenfield Village during the 1950s, eventually taught a class there. When the adult craft classes were temporarily discontinued, she opened her own studio—the Dearborn Handweaving Studio, located one mile from Greenfield Village—the only local source of weaving equipment, supplies, and instruction at the time. A 1960 *Warp and Weft* article stated that most of her students were "school teachers, nurses, housewives, and office workers" and that "her enthusiasm has infected her dozen and a half grandchildren . . . who weave at home."[25] As her studio was so close, she continued her association with the village.

Michigan Weavers Guild member Libby Crawford also recalled learning to weave at Greenfield Village. A neighbor asked her to go along to a class, and she agreed reluctantly, as she was busy raising a family and was not interested in weaving: "We went out to Greenfield Village to take weaving from Ida Gustafson, a Swedish woman who was teaching there at that time." Crawford enjoyed weaving from the start and ordered a small metal loom that she had seen in a magazine. When her "vegetable man" saw this loom, he told her about another woman in Detroit who taught weaving, so Crawford took lessons from her also. But Crawford maintained, "Ida was my mentor, as well as Gerhardt Knodel."[26] Knodel once taught a summer class at Cranbrook Academy of Art. Crawford joined the Michigan Weavers Guild when it was formed in 1947 and became a well-known and respected weaving teacher throughout the country and Canada. Guild member Nancy Peck also learned to weave at Greenfield Village, taking lessons in 1975. Peck had taken a class in spinning through the adult education program at the village and was fascinated. But she wanted to make the actual cloth, so she decided to try weaving and reports that she "was hooked with it after my first weaving class." Peck remembers: "Margaret McAllister, who is a member of Michigan Weavers Guild, was my instructor. And at that time they were doing day classes. They had a very active program . . . I was weaving down there nearly every day. Once you got past the beginning class, they had big floor looms and you could go in and take the next class—intermediate class. We were free to come and go . . . five days a week we could weave . . . eight hours a day, or however long we wanted to go. I really didn't have anything else to do at that time, so it was one of those things. I just was experimenting with all the different kinds of weaves. So I really jumped right into it."[27]

Students in the village program met upstairs at the Cotton Gin Mill, now the Weaving Building. Peck recalls: "The setup in the weaving building was unique in that the downstairs was open to the public to see the looms and sock knitting machines. The upstairs, not open to the public, housed the table and floor looms."[28] There were perhaps a dozen four-shaft floor looms and the same number of table looms, in various stages of repair/disrepair. Instructors and students spent a lot of time keeping them working. Peck had majored in textiles and related arts at Michigan State, but the school's weaving looms were reserved for interior decorating students: "I had spent years working through the various fiber arts: knitting, embroidery, needlepoint, and crochet. I have always sewn and felt there was more potential to use the finished handwoven product. I didn't realize all the possibilities that the [village] class would open for me."[29] When McAllister left, Peck was invited to take over the teaching. She felt she knew enough to teach the beginners, and she was eventually confident enough to take them on to the next level. "Thus began my weaving teaching career," says Peck, who taught from 1976 to 1986. Classes did not continue for long after she moved and had to give up teaching: "Attendance was up and down. Some sessions ran and some didn't. This was the mid-eighties and more women were going to work and didn't want to spend their evenings taking classes."[30]

In the Detroit area, the Detroit Institute of Arts (DIA) provided opportunities for weavers to exhibit in juried shows. A Detroit group of artists formed the Scarab Club, which worked with the DIA to organize exhibits beginning in 1910. Exhibits by Michigan Artists-Craftsmen were held at the DIA from 1947 through 1979, with Cranbrook tapestry weaver Lillian Holm receiving the first Founders Purchase Award, in 1949. The DIA also co-sponsored arts and crafts exhibits with other galleries in Michigan for large statewide shows in 1974–75 and 1980–81. These exhibits included works by professional handweavers as well as guild members. At the sixth annual exhibition, in 1951, Harriet Tidball, one of the four jurors for the show, was quoted in the fiber journal *Handweaver and Craftsman* as commenting "that the serious amateur in the field of weaving need have no fear of showing his work in competition with professionals."[31] The Detroit Artists Market, founded in 1932, has member artists and designers from the area and exhibits their work at their Detroit Cultural Center gallery.

Today, such organizations as the MLH, the Scarab Club, the Fiber Arts Network (FAN), and Michigan Surface Design Association offer juried textile shows, supporting the craft and art of handweaving and the fiber arts. The FAN is a Michigan-based, nonprofit organization dedicated to promoting and providing information about fiber-art activities among its members throughout the area. Founded in 2003, the FAN publishes four quarterly newsletters and sponsored its first juried biennial show, *New Fibers*, in 2004. Michigan's Surface Design Association, organized in 1977, sponsors workshops, demonstrations, and lectures.

African Americans in Detroit formed the Michigan chapter of the National Conference of Artists (NCA) in 1974 and held their first art show in 1986. The strength of their gallery, now in the Northwest Activities Center, attracts a broad range of member artists from Detroit and many other locations. The mission of this national organization—according to Shirley Woodson-Reid, Michigan NCA president, artist, and supervisor of art education for the city of Detroit—is "to preserve and support African American Culture through the visual arts," with exhibitions, lectures, tours, and special events, including fiber shows. Several African American weavers from Detroit—Najma Wilson, Elizabeth Youngblood, Valerie Fair, Sonya Clark, and Camille Ann Brewer—have had solo fiber shows at the gallery. All these weavers have fiber degrees from Michigan schools—Brewer from the University of Michigan, Clark and Youngblood from Cranbrook, Wilson from the College of Creative Studies, and Fair from Wayne State University. All are working artists, some in mixed media or painting with weaving. Clark, Youngblood, and Wilson also teach.[32]

For a few years in the 1980s and 1990s, the Ann Arbor Art Center offered weaving classes, often taught by graduate students at the University of Michigan. But these classes stopped in 1999 due to lack of space and funding, and the looms were stored. Earlier—from the 1960s until she died in 1980—Joyce Jones taught weaving (with Jane Hawkins) at the Ann Arbor YM-YWCA. Many of her students are still in the area and are active members of the Ann Arbor Fiberarts Guild. Charlene Hancock, an art rug weaver in Ann Arbor, reported: "For many years Joyce was weaving in Ann Arbor. She taught us all."[33] The MLH has a scholarship in Jones's name.

Yarn Shops Are Meccas

When the Handweavers Guild of America held its first convergence in Detroit in 1972, Linton Davidson of Old Mill Yarns in Eaton Rapids, south of Lansing, compiled a list of fifteen weaving and spinning supply shops in Michigan, most of which also offered classes. Most of these were located in the south-central portion of the state.[34] Only one of these remains in this business today—Old Mill Yarns. It not only offers a wide range of weaving and fiber-art equipment, as well as new and mill-end yarns, but also houses the MLF files and hosts the MLH board meetings. Today, all levels of weaving instruction are given there by Marilyn Kempf, Leslie Johnson, and Linda Griffith. In Ann Arbor, The Wild Weft served weavers with supplies, instruction, and exhibition space beginning in 1972. When it closed in 1985, Charles Botero decided to carry on the tradition and turned his design studio at Whitmore Lake into Forma, a weaving supply shop with classes taught by Ann Arbor weavers, including Charlene Hancock and Marj Mink. Classes there are currently taught by Sarah Kauffman, a professional, award-winning artist who graduated from Eastern Michigan University with an MFA and exhibits in American Crafts Council shows.

New shops have opened, offering weaving, spinning, and knitting supplies and other fiber-art materials, as well as instruction. North of Eaton Rapids, fiber artist Nancy McRay, who studied with Sherri Smith at the University of Michigan, offers classes in weaving and other fiber arts at Woven Art, her shop in East Lansing. All levels of weaving are taught by Betty Forsythe and Gisela Bosch at The Spinning Loft in Howell, as well as by Julie Anderson at her business in the Grand Rapids area, the Threadbender Yarn Shop. The Heritage Spinning and Weaving shop in Lake Orion opened in 2000 and offers beginning and continuing classes, plus workshops from well-known teachers. Owner Joan Sheridan Hoover is a weaver, spinner, dyer, knitter, and felter, and she has a background in marketing.

Her shop in the northern Detroit suburbs has a dedicated dye workshop, a classroom, and a sitting room. Until the late 1990s, Gloria Teeter provided a similar refuge at Traditional Handicrafts in Northville (west of Detroit), where her customers could find the most recent fibers and equipment. Teeter also provided beginning and continuing instruction. Today, her shop is located in Canadian Lakes, Michigan. In Marquette, fiber artists can visit Town Folk Gallery, owned by Sandy Belt, which has the latest yarn and instructions for knitting and crochet, as well as new novelty yarns and lots of books. Also in Marquette, the shop Uncommon Threads features many classes and workshops, as well as yarns and books. Its owner, Donna Cowhide, helps organize a free yearly "Knit-Out and Crochet Too" event at the local arts center, to teach people how to knit.[35]

Weaving needs have been well supplied in Michigan for decades through the efforts of the art centers and local shops, which still often function as informal centers of information and reliable instruction opportunities. Every fiber artist knows the appeal of browsing through the yarn bins, where touching is not only permitted but encouraged. Having shops within driving distance (at least in the southern portion of the state) is considered a boon.

SEVEN

Trends of the Times

The state of handweaving and the fiber arts in Michigan today is the result of the interaction of many influences, individuals, and events. Art and craft are not created in a vacuum. The events and concerns of the larger society often create a context from which artists and craftspeople take their inspirations. Eunice Anders of the Michigan Weavers Guild emphasized, "Things we produce are really an outgrowth from everything we've done and experienced, and read, and seen."[1] The unique contributions of individual weavers in Michigan in the period from 1930 to the present reflect trends in the arts and crafts.

The 1930s: Revitalizing Traditional Handweaving

During the depression years of the 1930s, Michigan handweaving was practiced in some communities by ethnic groups, such as the Finns, as a traditional craft. With the exception of pockets of practicing home weavers who passed down their knowledge within the family and community, the skills of weaving were taught by very few. A new or prospective weaver could, however, learn by taking lessons in such places as Cromaine Crafts at Hartland, beginning in 1934 with Osma Gallinger and later with Martina Lindahl. Although spinning and knowledge of working with unspun fibers were somewhat lost skills at this time, Martina Lindahl was an excellent spinner who brought these skills to Hartland from her native Sweden. She was so proficient at spinning that "Cranbrook students came to learn from her."[2]

Gradually, Greenfield Village in Detroit and a few other areas around the state offered weaving lessons. Some colleges offered weaving instruction in departments of occupational therapy, home economics, and art education. Or one could become self-taught by correspondence through a subscription to Mary Atwater's *Shuttle-Craft Bulletin*. The new weaver would learn to warp and thread a loom, read a weaving draft, and practice the skills of weaving textiles in traditional patterns using fine cottons, linens, and wools.

Those who mastered the craft often found themselves passing along that knowledge. During this period, Latin teacher Muriel Neeland was weaving after school and in the summers. She also taught weaving to some neighbors and children in Mancelona, including seventh grader Anne Westlund, who continued weaving into adulthood. Neeland's friend Loretta Nichols was also weaving, making fine textiles, garments, and purses. As an occupational therapist, Nichols taught weaving to patients at the state hospital in Traverse City.[3]

The 1940s: New Postwar Materials

During the years of World War II, fashion and styles were practical, and many materials were scarce because of war needs. In this stressful time, Kay Holman, a member of Marquette's Blue Pots guild, learned to cope and create as a new weaver. She maintains: "You can't just say weaving is making something out of nothing. It's more than that. As you work, you see color and patterns growing. And all by putting one thread together at a time."[4]

After the war ended in 1945, styles changed. The "contemporary" look was sleek, functional, pared down. Returning GIs and their wives were creating the new "baby boomer" generation (1946–64). There was a demand for housing and a boom in building as new families resumed peacetime living. Arthur Levitt built low-cost quality housing, developing the first Levittown in Hempstead, Long Island. New textiles—rugs, draperies, and furnishings—were needed for the new homes. In this environment, weavers were beginning to experiment with new designs and ideas, while relying on the traditions of the past. New man-made fibers were explored and used by the "modern" weaver and in industry. Dorothy Liebes in San Francisco was one of the first American weavers to experiment with metallics, wood, and novelty textured fibers in bright colors for screens and other contemporary textiles. Loraine Kessenich, of the Kessenich Loom Company in Wisconsin, a frequent participant in Michigan conferences, was noted for her experiments with the new Darvan fiber for the B. F. Goodrich Company. She wove several projects with synthetic fibers, including a mitral heart valve woven of synthetics and fine silk threaded at four hundred ends per inch.[5]

For the handweaver, the emphasis in weaving continued to focus on structure. Most woven items were functional—textiles for the home or yardage for clothing. Demand for these goods was high because commercial looms had been devoted to war items. As Alice Waagen points out in *An Historical Survey and Analysis of American Handweaving*, at the end of the war, "people found themselves faced with consumer products that had been designed ten to fifteen years earlier. . . . [and] there [now] was a demand for new and innovative products."[6] Also, women who had entered the workforce during and after the war had more spending income for the hobby of weaving. The yarns used in weaving were still the fine natural fibers of cotton, linen, and wool, plus the added novelty of new postwar synthetics—rayons and then nylon.

In the late 1940s, educational opportunities were newly available to the returning soldier through the GI Bill of Rights, which provided "great incentive and support for colleges and universities to expand art departments and develop new craft programs."[7] Ceramics and textiles were seen as important arts, and these schools were now attracting artists of the highest caliber to teach.[8] Many of these teachers were refugees from the war-torn Europe of the 1930s and 1940s. They instilled in their students the design ideologies of Scandinavia and the Bauhaus. In 1941, Anni Albers was teaching in North Carolina at Black Mountain College (1933–49). She brought new ideas, advocating that handweavers avoid repeating traditional patterns and look to fundamental principles as a base for imagining and freely developing new textile forms. She advised students to work with the material and react to it.[9] Mary Atwater criticized these ideas for art in weaving and reaffirmed the importance of well-constructed and useful textiles.[10] But the Bauhaus approach of creating well-designed pieces with an understanding of the nature of the materials being used and of the application of the designs to mass production became widely accepted by professional weavers and art schools. However, most handweavers—guild members or hobbyists—believed in weaving traditional patterns, with some experimentation.

College-trained weavers and fiber artists, such as David Van Dommelen, a textile artist and professor at Pennsylvania State University who received his MA from Michigan State University in 1956, "differed from the self taught craftsperson by being exposed to a variety of information" and new ideas. He recalled, "When I got out of the army I went back to Michigan State . . . And that's where I really began to be influenced by people like Alma Getch and Catherine Winkler and the faculty. . . ."[11] Karl Laurell, who was commissioned in 1950 by the Grand Rapids Furniture Museum to design and weave casement material for one entire wall of a room, was "a veteran who turned craftsman." He had spent four years aboard a U.S. Navy destroyer in World War II and then enrolled in art courses. Working in art "became a consuming interest" and led him to study at the School for American Craftsmen in Rochester, New York, where he specialized in weaving.[12] Such new educational opportunities, available through the GI Bill of Rights, encouraged and created new weavers and fiber artists.

In the fall of 1947, a new center for the production of handweaving was opened in the Detroit metropolitan area. In that year, noted eye surgeon Dr. Ralph Pino of Detroit founded Plymouth Colony Farms in Plymouth, Michigan, with the idea of combining agriculture and the crafts. The first craft center he established was the handweaving center, whose products were soon featured in the Detroit area. "Unusually beautiful upholstery fabric designed by Mrs. Antoinette Webster of the Farms" was exhibited at the Detroit Institute of Arts in 1949, and linens "attracted the attention at the 17th Annual Housewares Exposition at the J. L. Hudson Company" in Detroit in January 1950.[13] In July 1951, artist-craftsman Karl Laurell assumed directorship of the weaving shops, carrying on the ideals of the founder and "providing many Americans with fabrics of good design and quality at a fair price."[14]

The 1950s: The Good Times

The Eisenhower years are remembered for peaceful good times and a return to normal life, but the 1950s also brought serious social challenges to the status quo: television, McCarthyism, the Korean War, civil rights protests, desegregated schools (*Brown v. Board of Education*, 1954), and Sputnik. The era was one of growth and excitement for the handicrafts in the United States. In 1949, the New York Museum of Modern Art exhibited the work of Anni Albers. This was its first showing of an individual textile artist, and the exhibit traveled for three years. The American Craftsmen's Educational Council (renamed American Craftsmen's Council in 1955 and American Craft Council in 1979) had formed in 1943, launched *Craft Horizons* magazine in 1948, and opened the Museum of Contemporary Crafts in 1956 (renamed the Museum of Arts and Design in 2005). These events gave new standing and visibility to contemporary crafts.[15] The Young American Craftsmen exhibits began in 1950, sponsored by the ACEC, providing a national showcase for the work of a new generation. The big department stores and specialty design shops displayed the works of modern designers from Scandinavia and the United States. *Handweaver and Craftsman* magazine started in 1950. Dorothy Liebes moved her design studio to New York City, and Jack Lenor Larsen established his design office there in 1951. In 1955, Lili Blumenau, who started the weaving department at the Fashion Institute of Technology in 1952, published her book *The Art and Craft of Hand Weaving*, which covered all the basics of handweaving and added a strong chapter on design.[16] As Jack Lenor Larsen recalls, when he came to New York from Cranbrook in 1951, it was a time when anything was possible—like "starting from zero and creating something totally new."[17] Larsen said: "The greatest change from traditional to contemporary weaving has been the emergence of the weaver as an individual. Because weaving is again in a creative phase it can become a studio art, a self-contained reality at once personalized and universal."[18]

Many Michigan weavers who became prominent in the state—such as Gampers members Mary Sayler of Grand Rapids; Eunice Anders of Leamington, Ontario; Mildred Dexter and Beatrice Larsen of Lansing; and Libby

Crawford of Detroit—were learning their craft at this time. Others were already teaching and selling their work. Gladys Rogers Brophil (Wonnacott) of Baldwin, a former owner of Norwood Loom Company and first editor of *Warp and Weft* (a monthly bulletin published by the Norwood Loom Company beginning in 1947), was teaching weaving. Mary Sayler took her first lessons with Brophil. Melvina McGarr, a later owner of Norwood Loom Company and founder of Nor'craft Weavers Guild, began giving lessons at the company craft shop in the early 1950s. She and her husband, Wallace, became charter members of the MLH. In Muskegon, Ruth Cross and her father were weaving fine garments and textiles; further south, Ruth Scherer, who owned a weaving studio in Niles, was teaching and conducting workshops in spinning, dyeing, and weaving. In Hudson, near the Ohio border, along U.S. Route 127, Hallco Hand Weavers, owned by Florence Hall and Louise Cornes, was producing lovely textiles for the home.[19]

The Griswolds: Production Weaving and Reproductions

Alice Griswold of East Lansing, whose work is known nationally, was beginning to explore weaving in 1951. "You have to perfect your craft first," she said, "and the sales will follow."[20] And they did. By the mid-1950s, Alice and her husband, Howard, were both involved in their growing weaving business. Needing a wider and faster loom, they bought a fifty-six-inch Macomber fly-shuttle loom. Soon after that, they bought a forty-eight-inch power loom from an old mill in Pennsylvania and a second one from the old Horner Woolen Mill in Eaton Rapids, Michigan.[21] Alice worked out prototypes on her small hand looms, with the limitations of the power looms always in mind, in order to achieve the quality of fabric desired. "It was a wonderful partnership," Alice said, "because Howard was so mechanically minded and intrigued with the operation of the power loom."[22] Alice designed the warps, and Howard kept the looms in operation.

The Griswolds' work was immediately in demand. They wove commissioned yardage for garments and household furnishings; afghans, stoles, and scarves for corporate custom-made Christmas gifts; and reproduction blankets and textiles for national park exhibits and museums across the country, including the Ellis Island restoration project and the Father Marquette Museum in Saint Ignace, Michigan. Reproduction pieces were produced after months of research about the fibers, dyes, and weave structure that came closest in reconstructing an original piece. In 1957, three of their textiles toured in a Smithsonian Institution show featuring Midwest designer-craftspeople, and in 1966, they were a part of the *Draperies for Art* tour.[23] One of their reproduction blankets is in the Smithsonian Archives.

Alice Griswold, *right*, with Black Sheep Weavers' Fiber Guild member Gisela
Bosch, at a guild meeting where Griswold spoke about her life experiences as a
weaver, October 2002. (Photo by Nadine Cloutier. Courtesy of the Black Sheep
Weavers' Fiber Guild.)

In the 1980s, Alice Griswold began leading workshops, giving lectures, and teaching. Early in her weaving career, she and Karin Haakonsen
translated Malin Selander's *Weaving Patterns from Sweden* (published in
Gothenburg, Sweden, in 1961). In 2000, Griswold published *Weaving Solutions*, "addressing [the] many problems needing solutions" that she experienced during her years of weaving.[24] At the 2002 MLH conference,
Griswold received an MLH Lifetime Service Award, in recognition of fifty
years of weaving. The award was a way to thank her for her sharing of weaving information—not only as a teacher, but also with weavers individually
—and recognized her as a professional weaver. Griswold, a member of a
number of guilds in Michigan, is also a member of the nationally and internationally recognized group Cross Country Weavers. She remains active
today, weaving and working on a new book based on three-shaft weaves.

The 1960s: The Natural Look

The Michigan League of Handweavers, which organized in the summer of
1959, began in an era of challenge. John F. Kennedy inspired a new generation, and his death shocked the nation. Politically, it was the turbulent
time of the Vietnam War, protests and the peace movement, urban riots,

and the women's movement. The nation was experiencing the flower children, pop art, Andy Warhol, the Beatles, and Mick Jagger. Betty Friedan's book *The Feminine Mystique* was challenging the status of women and rocking the standing of professions—such as home economics—that were associated with house and home. There was also intense interest in the sciences and ethnic cultures of the world. By 1969, the United States had landed on the moon.

Weaving and fiber arts were impacted by these events as well as by the "Back to Earth" environmental movement, with its teach-ins and concerns about pollution and waste. Favored yarns for weaving were handspun and hand dyed from natural materials. The fiber look was bulky, loopy, large. Wall art made of woven fibers incorporated weeds, shells, and other natural objects. Handwoven garments, such as the popular poncho, were fringed, looped, and shaped on the loom. Woven clothing no longer had the sleek 1950s look but, rather, reflected cultural sensitivities to clothing as related to natural environments and other cultures. Weavers and fiber artists were discovering textiles and clothing in other cultures at home and abroad—often through travel, study, or work in the Peace Corps. Dorothy Franz, a member of the guild Friends of the Fleece, joined the Peace Corps in 1967 when she was sixty-four. While in Africa, she worked with weavers in Chad and Tunisia; she returned with many textiles and new cultural traditions to share with her community in the Port Sanilac area.[25]

Dottie Goodwin of the Weavers Guild of Kalamazoo recalls the experience of being a new weaver in these exciting times: "When I got interested in weaving, it was in the Sixties. And I think that influenced what we pursued right at the start. It was the peace movement! Hand made, hand woven clothing was in. Ponchos and tunics were big—and those were good pieces to start weaving on."[26] Guild members were weaving the new styles in clothing, and guilds were presenting a variety of programs to their memberships, with such topics as weave and wear, handbags, tie-dyeing, yarn dyeing, Finnish lace, tartans, and shadow weave. Harriet Tidball's move back to Michigan in 1959 to care for her sick father gave Michigan weavers' groups a new energy and focus. Her niece remembers handwoven textiles everywhere in Tidball's home, which was "extremely modern . . . in a lot of ways," with "Danish style furniture from the early Sixties with that warm wood and the natural forms," and "all of the upholstery was hand woven or chosen specifically for its color and its texture."[27] Throughout this period, Tidball brought world-renowned weavers to Michigan and other areas of the United States to promote textiles for the home and office and clothing.

The sciences and medicine were inspiring new work. In 1964, at Cranbrook Academy of Art, Glen Kaufman, head of the department of weaving and textile design, was continuing the Cranbrook tradition of working with industry, designing and consulting for the General Motors "Art in Research" program. Through this program, Kaufman was creating textiles

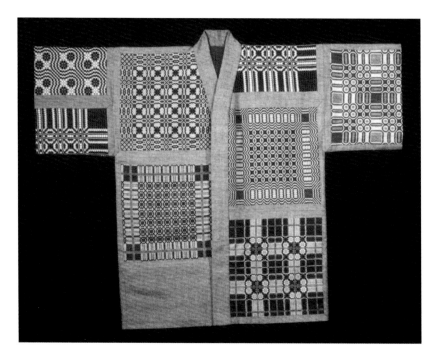

Front of a kimono designed and constructed by JoAnn Bachelder from squares handwoven of wool and cotton in traditional overshot patterns by members of a Midland FiberArts Guild study group (Meg Alstatter, JoAnn Bachelder, Joan Catacosinos, Betty Dailey, Susan Dudzik, Vi Friedrich, Sue Peters, Louise Speier, Jean Stanwick, Julia Steinmetz, Maggie Thurber, and Ruth Tomlinson), ca. 1985. (Photo by Pearl Yee Wong. Courtesy of the Michigan State University Museum.)

that highlighted the work that scientists were doing, bringing art and research together before the public. Kaufman worked closely with the GM scientists to develop fabric designs from their microphotographs, both those in color and atomic models. The results were shown at the *Art in Research* exhibit at the New York World's Fair.[28]

The 1970s: Fiber Art Arrives

The Nixon years culminated in Watergate, the downfall of a president, and a brief time for healing. The United States was attempting affirmative action for minorities to remedy past discrimination. The Supreme Court upheld *Roe v. Wade*, affirming a woman's right to abortion. An energy crisis, inflation, and the Iranian holding of American hostages added to the pressure. The fiber arts movement, which would soon grow and expand, was in its infancy. Art broke loose from the loom "to grow in size and scale, to move off the wall into three-dimensional physicality."[29] In 1973, an important book, *Beyond Craft: The Art Fabric*, by Mildred Constantine and Jack

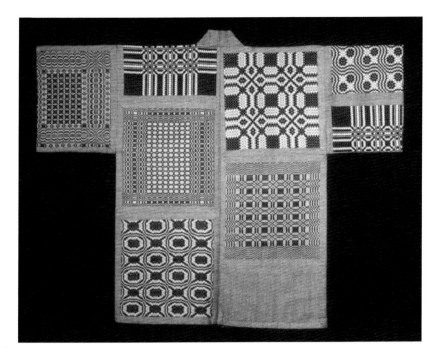

Back of the kimono made by members of the Midland FiberArts Guild, ca. 1985. (Photo by Pearl Yee Wong. Courtesy of the Michigan State University Museum.)

Lenor Larsen, gave everyone a look at the new work in fibers that had been appearing in exhibits and craft magazines.[30] But what was the focus of the movement: art fabric, fiber art, textile art? It included large handwoven architectural installations, handwoven art clothing, hand-wrapped and hand-knotted art for the wall, and three-dimensional sculptural forms. Mixing techniques and materials was common.

When Gerhardt Knodel arrived from California in 1970 as artist-in-residence to lead the fiber department at Cranbrook Academy of Art, the department was already in transition. Strengell had retired in 1961, and her successors, Glen Kaufman and Robert Kidd, had introduced rya (tufted) works and sculptural fiber-art pieces. Novelty fibers, such as wood and metal slats, were used by Cranbrook artist Robert Sailors. The bright California colors and metallics associated with the work of Dorothy Liebes were welcome in the CAA studios. "The students in the seventies were in strong revolt against tapestry as the only form of art weaving," Knodel recalls. New ideas presented in the new books and exhibitions and postwar sculptural work from Poland influenced Knodel's own experiments with the creation of fiber environments.[31] Knodel was commissioned to fill the atrium space for the Plaza Hotel in Detroit's new Renaissance Center in 1977. *Free Fall*, a series of forty curved fabric planes, hung suspended by Plexiglas tubes, nylon rope, and steel cable in the seventy-foot multistory opening. The

King Neptune, a handwoven mask with crocheted curls by Ruth Whitmyer, 1983. (Photo courtesy of the Mill Race Weavers Guild.)

gold, bronze, and white fabrics swayed and shimmered in the air currents, warming the concrete and wood structure. Knodel is noted for his fiber environments and for work that relates to unique architectural spaces.[32] Works of fiber were sought after. Architects and builders wanted them in their buildings. Detroit weaver Eleanor Safford wrote a full-page article about all the fiber work in the Renaissance Center in a late 1970s MLH newsletter: "Of the 29 works commissioned by John Portman and Associates, the developer of Detroit's Renaissance Center, 17 are sculpture and painting and twelve are fiber works . . . The majority of the fiber pieces are within the hotel itself . . . For the most part the colors are warm and soften the hard concrete walls." Safford describes the works by Michigan fiber artists Susan Aaron-Taylor, Diane Barr, James Gilbert, Robert Kidd, Jane Knight, Gerhardt Knodel, and Sherri Smith.

At the same time, the nation's bicentennial focus on colonial America spurred renewed interest in weaving and crafts. Some guilds returned to a study of traditional weaving; members of study groups wove and exchanged hand towels and squares for "friendship coverlets" in overshot patterns. Other guilds explored new ideas, thinking of fibers as an art form and exploring new techniques in surface treatment and dyeing. In Traverse City, Northland Weavers members Terry Tarnow and Martha Fox constructed a woven textile web on the porch of a Main Street building and invited the community to weave. Technology and computer-drafted patterns were in greater use. A new group of fiber artists headed weaving programs in Michigan colleges and universities. Shop owners had the worry of loss of fibers supplied by third world countries because of the scare and threat of anthrax. Jochen Ditterich recalls a time in the late 1970s when his business suffered a substantial loss as a result of the scare: "There was a big article in the newspaper: 'Small Time Weaver in California Died of Anthrax' . . . [and then] the health department came in and took five hundred pounds of goat's hair . . . It was a big loss."[33] Weavers were purchasing and using these exotic fibers in unusual ways; guilds were offering programs and workshops to members in new interest areas: ikat, crochet and wrapped sculpture, painted warps, indigo dyeing, off-loom weaving, felting, surface design (in workshops entitled "Fold and Dye" and "Hot Acid Dyeing"), and more.

Art-to-Wear Takes a Front Seat

At the beginning of the seventies, clothing styles were in transition, ranging from the miniskirt, to hot pants and boots, to the maxicoat. Handwoven garments that were tubular and constructed on the loom were new and exciting. There was hardly anyone nationwide weaving and constructing clothing that was an expression of this new art. However, in Michigan, Rosalind "Roz" Berlin and Barbara Wittenberg were introducing new ideas in garments and design. Berlin, a young weaver in the late 1960s and early 1970s, received wide attention with her earth-toned garments woven and shaped on the loom, featured at the HGA convergence in 1972. Today, Berlin creates "tree of life" forms that are tubular woven and have evolved from her work in the mid-1970s. Her solo installations feature beautiful environmental sculptured "forests" in arrays of colors. Berlin's vision has been to "weave a sacred grove of the four seasons, bringing us back to the earth."[34] She has also said of the woven forest, "When I create my trees, I seek to touch the ancient memory core of all who walk within the forest, to

This grouping of trees, with young dancers from the Concord Academy of Antrim who performed during the opening ceremony of the installation "Fantasy Forest: A Room-Sized Woven Environment," was exhibited at The Crooked Tree Art Center in Petoskey, Michigan, January 2005. The trees, handwoven by Roz Berlin, are a blend of natural and synthetic fibers woven in the tubular method. (Photo © G. Randall Goss.)

somehow increase an awareness and perhaps alter how we think or feel about our inner and outer worlds."[35] Since the 1970s, she has been active teaching weaving, lecturing, and exhibiting.

There was a renewed interest in tapestries during the 1970s, too: the Smithsonian Institution toured an exhibit of exquisite tapestries by the child weavers of Harrania, Egypt. Georgia Bick taught tapestry to many Michigan weavers at this time. Bick was French and schooled in tapestry weaving in Europe. She married an American from Michigan who was in the U.S. Air Force during World War II. She and her husband settled in Michigan, where Bick continued her tapestry work and teaching. She did repairs and restoration of the tapestries at the Metropolitan Museum of Art in New York City and was on the board of the Toledo Museum of Art. Her work appeared in several juried shows in Michigan.

Also during this period, many Michigan guild members became prominent weavers and fiber artists. Ethel Alexander of the Greater Lansing Weavers Guild, whose specialty was designing place mats to coordinate with china, lectured and taught weaving workshops. Martha Brownscombe, president of the MLH from 2003 to 2005 and an award-winning weaver

Loom-shaped cotton mini-dress with a warp-wrapped midriff and shoulders by Kati Meek, 1970. (Photo by Pearl Yee Wong. Courtesy of the Michigan State University Museum.)

whose works are often inspired by objects from nature, learned to weave at Michigan State University during the 1970s. She studied with Joanne Eichert for her MA. Brownscombe did her research in textiles in Africa, and some of her early work was inspired by African weaving patterns and styles. Kati Reeder Meek began weaving in 1970. As a new weaver, she had purchased one hundred pounds of cotton and decided to make a long warp. Her first project—an orange loom-shaped minidress with a warp-wrapped midriff and shoulders—reflects the style and colors of the time. Meek calls it her "daring dress." When she moved to Alpena, she helped found the Northeast Michigan Weavers Guild. Today, Meek is known for her work with fine linens, precise tartans, long-eyed heddles, and the drawloom. As a teacher and writer, Meek has researched and uses many traditional patterns based on Lithuanian weaving, which she shares in her new book *Reflections from a Flaxen Past: For Love of Lithuanian Weaving.*[36]

Chris Triola, a Michigan State University graduate in art education, taught high school art and became interested in weaving and design when her students wanted to learn to use the large loom in the classroom. Through the 1970s and 1980s, Triola lectured and led workshops on the creative process and the designing of handwoven textiles. She designed, manufactured, and marketed her own clothing line, inspired by the world around her. Triola has shifted her focus/direction to knitted garments, which are created in Lansing in her factory, Chris Triola Productions, with a staff of full-time employees and Michigan State University interns. Chris Triola studios are found in galleries throughout Michigan and the country. Triola serves on the board of trustees of the American Craft Council.[37]

The 1980s: Technology and Complexity

President Ronald Reagan returned the United States to a focus on old-style conservative values, tax cuts, and domestic spending cuts. But the defense budget and the deficit grew. The first cases of AIDS became public. By the end of the decade, President George Bush Sr. had engaged the United States in the 1990 Gulf War.

Weaving design and technology were taking new directions. In the March/April 1982 issue of *Fiberarts*, which was beginning its second decade, editor Joanne Mattera discussed the magazine's decision to devote the issue to machines (the power loom, the Jacquard loom, computer-aided looms): "We're excited about it and plan to have more articles on artists who dip into the technological well, some maintaining involvement with the tradition that inspired them, others rushing full speed ahead into industrial processes and techniques."[38] From the mid-1980s forward, there was an expanded interest in complex woven structures, patterning, and surface design. Garments were constructed with more finishing and refinement. Fine yarns and threads were being used. Complex multiple-shaft looms were in greater use, as were software programs for designing handwovens. "Computer-interfaced looms were first introduced at Convergence 1982 in Seattle," Margaret Windeknecht said, adding, "Both AVL and Macomber showed them that year." The following year, the Macomber version was shown at the MLH conference. According to Windeknecht, for the multishaft weaver, computer interface "has been a great boon!" One can see why. As Windeknecht explains, "The computer interface essentially gives an unlimited number of treadles, allows them to be used in a sequence far too complicated to remember, and eliminates the necessity of tying the treadles (often done at ground level) or pegging a dobby chain."[39]

Windeknecht, a well-known Michigan weaver and author, has explored a wide range of techniques. In 1973, she wove the batik *Eye to Eye with a Fly* for *Shuttle Spindle and Dyepot*'s first color cover. Windeknecht often enjoys using humor in her weavings and works with computer technology to accomplish weaving goals. She has published six books, the most noted being *Color-and-Weave* (1981), which broke new ground in handweaving. It was published jointly with her husband, Thomas, who designed, constructed, and programmed the computer graphics for the extensive study leading to this book. During the following summer, at the 1982 HGA convergence, Windeknecht led seminars on computer-aided design for the four-shaft and multishaft looms, and conducted a two-day workshop on color-and-weave. In 1983, Windeknecht had a stroke that left her without the use of her right hand, but she pursues her weaving, continuing to win awards. The computer gives her the opportunity to continue writing and, beginning in 1987, to self-publish.[40]

Verda Elliott points out that weaving equipment had become "more sophisticated" in the eighties. When she first started weaving, there were no dobby looms available "and certainly no computer interface—no computer-aided design." She concludes, "Just as the world has become more technologically advanced, so has weaving."[41] Elliott, who taught weaving at the Birmingham Bloomfield Art Center and is a past president of the MLH, became very interested in computer-assisted designing and taught workshops in using this tool for weaving. During the workshop she gave at the 1990 MLH conference, Elliott said that she had purchased her first computer in 1983 and that it "changed both my life and my work as a weaver."[42] She is an award-winning artist and has written frequently for weaving magazines.

Guilds and individuals were not only working with new techology and designing capabilities but were also looking to the past for inspiration. In the mid-1980s, Michigan was planning its sesquicentennial celebration. For this celebration in 1987, the study group of the Greater Lansing Weavers Guild researched the history and weaving of ethnic groups that were a major part of Michigan's population during the first fifty years of statehood. Each researcher wrote the history of her chosen ethnic group and wove samples of a traditional or typical pattern or structure to share with other group members. The ethnic groups studied were African American, English, Finnish, French Canadian, German, Irish, Michigan American Indian, Scottish, and Swedish. A copy of the resulting notebook was made for the library of the Greater Lansing Weavers Guild (as is customary for projects of the guild's study group), and the results of the research and weaving were exhibited in the Lansing Public Main Library.

Sharing Their Talents

Prominent Michigan guild weavers and fiber artists during the 1980s who have each served as president of the MLH are Patti Aiken, JoAnn Bachelder,

The Presence of Absence Is Every-where, a wall hanging hand-woven of wools, cottons, silk, rayon, and metallics by Kathy Zasuwa in the style of Theo Moorman, 2001. (Photo courtesy of Kathy Zasuwa.)

Charlene Hancock, Lestra Hazel, Priscilla Lynch, Brenda Mergen, Sue Peters, and Kathy Zasuwa. Aiken, an award-winning weaver, gave workshops in her specialty, ikat. She is an accomplished writer, with an interest in the history of weaving in Michigan, particularly Hartland. Bachelder, a former instructor at the Midland Center for the Arts, continues to teach traditional weave structures and free-form design at her studio and in workshops. Early in her weaving career, Bachelder wove yardage, constructed art wear, and led workshops in sewing with handwoven cloth. Today, her wall hangings, originally inspired by Nancy Searles's *Techniques of Freeform Design* (1984), go beyond free form—achieving multilayers of form through weave structure and dyeing techniques. Hancock, a prize-winning fiber artist, specialized in art rugs; she led workshops in such techniques as pick and pick (alternating colors to form verticle stripes) rug weaving and also taught at the Forma weaving supply shop. Hazel excels in rep weaves and functional fibers. Her work has been included frequently in *Handwoven's* design series, as have articles she has written for the magazine. She was featured for a time in the magazine's ads for the Schacht hand loom. Lynch has specialized in award-winning handwoven garments and tapestries.

Mergen was a production weaver for many years and has taught workshops and specializes in woven and embellished garments, particularly sweaters and jackets. Peters is a weaver of fine functional textiles and uses computer software as a design tool in creating original specialty pieces on her twenty-four-shaft loom. Zasuwa is an accomplished weaver who lectures, teaches, and exhibits. Through her weavings, she continues and expands the pioneering work of Theo Moorman, using the characteristic multilayered inlay style in her work.

Millie Danielson is a much respected weaver and teacher in many techniques, particularly design, tapestry, liturgical textiles, and weaving with copper wire. She has received awards for her dramatic art-to-wear clothing and wall hangings and receives many commissions from corporations and churches for her award-winning tapestries. Carole Furtado, one of few production weavers in Michigan, began her classic line of wool and mohair scarves, vests, hats, and woven jewelry by selling in street fairs and now sells in several galleries and has a Web site. She is currently exploring surface embellishments and felting. Finnish American Johanna Pohjala, a rug weaver from the Upper Penninsula, well known for her beautiful and inventive rag rugs, received the Lifetime Achievement Award in 2000 from the Yarnwinders Fiber Guild, for her craftsmanship as a weaver and dedication as a guild member.

The 1990s: A New Century Coming

The Berlin Wall had fallen in 1989, and Germany was unified in 1990. The Clinton years brought improvements in the market and a reduction of the national deficit, but he was dogged by partisan strife and scandal. Turning the century mark was easy, but what came next was a watershed for the nation: September 11, 2001, followed by a second war in Iraq.

The 1990s brought a renewal of interest in natural fibers and fiber animals. Michigan fiber artists were incorporating into their weaving the exotic fibers of llama, alpaca, and buffalo; others were raising these animals and spinning their fibers. Textiles and handweaving moved in newer directions in the 1990s; artists were experimenting with a wide range of techniques, and the public was responding positively. Quilting had been enjoying a renaissance starting in the 1980s, and quilts became art for the wall. Exploration of ikat and shibori dyeing techniques and differential shrinkage and felting gave weavers new territory to explore. Organizations that had started as groups of weavers opened to all fiber artists, and the lines between art, craft, and design were hazier than ever. The Friends of Fiber Art International (1991) was founded to educate the public about collecting fiber art. By the end of the decade, *SOFA (Sculptural Objects and Functional Art)* opened in Chicago in 1994, and its sister show opened in New

Joetta Brady paints her warp with dyes prepared earlier in the day during a workshop, October 2000. (Photo by Nadine Cloutier. Courtesy of the Black Sheep Weavers' Fiber Guild.)

York City in 1998.[43] Works in fiber were accepted in some art galleries and art exhibitions without being separated into a craft designation.

Weaving a New Century

Today's weavers and fiber artists in Michigan continue to explore, experiment, and share new techniques through exhibiting and also by publishing their work. Mary Gleason Best's article on six-shaft shadow weave done in color blocks for a vest appeared in *Handwoven* in March 2005. Sarah Kauffman, who teaches at Forma, has been published in volume 6 of *Fiberarts Design Book*. Marion T. Marzolf, past president of the MLH, began writing articles about fiber artists in 2000 and has been published in *Fiberarts* and *Shuttle Spindle and Dyepot*. Stefanie Meisel of Grass Lake, who is self-taught and has gone twice for classes at Penland School of Crafts, has written four articles for *Handwoven* beginning in the spring of 2003, exploring new techniques and materials. Holly Shaltz of Boyne City published "Weaving with Singles: One Spinner's Journey," in *Spinoff*'s spring 2002 issue.

Felting is the medium that inspires Loretta Oliver today. In her studio in Detroit, she makes a variety of felted items, ranging from three-fingered mittens, "purse-onality" bags, scarves, clothing, small vessels, and wall hangings. Oliver creates scarves and yardage with wonderfully curved edges, one of her design signatures, by felting wool to loosely woven pieces. Her works, often playful, have won prizes in several national competitions. Oliver teaches at Wayne State University in Detroit, where she received her MA in fibers in 1998. She has taught about fibers in art classes at Adrian College and teaches workshops—in several felting techniques—across the country. She credits Michigan artist Kathy Zasuwa as the teacher who introduced her to felting in a workshop.[44]

Jill Ault, who has won many awards for her quilts and has a BFA from Eastern Michigan University, has taken quilting and piecing to a new level, using the technique of Korean *pojagi* (pieced wrapping cloths) in her silk organza wall art. She cuts and stitches fabric pieces together, creating complex layered patterns. Sometimes her work is adorned with feathers, beads, or other small metal objects and enhanced with shibori patterning and other dyeing techniques. Ann Schumacher, who received her MFA in fibers from Cranbrook Art Academy and was associate professor of textiles and design at Berea College in Kentucky between 1985 and 1995, excels in tapestry. She moved to Michigan and now works as a full-time studio artist. Her award-winning work is noted for the subtle use of color blending and abstract expressionism and appears in volumes 5, 6, and 7 of *Fiberarts Design Book.*

Fiber artists are crossing the old boundaries between art and functional craft. There is a blossoming of new work in a wide range of techniques, representing the skillful use of new dyeing techniques, the computer, creative stitchery, felting, beading, basketry, and paper weaving. Outstanding works in traditional tapestry, rugs, and useful objects for the home are exhibited with the new work. Fiber art is expressive, personalized, and often political. While the spotlight is often on the quest for the newest developments, it is important to note that high standards of craftsmanship and respect for materials and appreciation for the foundations of the crafts and their traditions seem to be gaining attention in the new century.

EIGHT

Weavers Organize
The MLH and the HGA

Twenty years after the first national weaving conference at Waldenwoods in Hartland, Michigan, a small group of women gathered at the former Cromaine Crafts Center in 1958 with the idea of forming a statewide organization. There were regional guilds in California and New England that may have served as models.[1] The idea of cooperation between guilds in Michigan had been discussed at a panel session of the Detroit Handweavers Tenth Anniversary Program in April 1958.[2] Participants suggested a variety of benefits that might come from some form of collaboration: sharing of lecturers and travel exhibitions, exchanging study group projects, smaller guilds gaining experience from larger ones. They also proposed an annual show and sale of work, a fashion show and demonstrations, a bulletin, an annual workshop or conference or seminar, and a permanent exhibition. The follow-up meeting, attended by ten interested weavers, was held in November of that year at Hartland Area Crafts to discuss a proposed Michigan state organization of handweavers.[3] Since the participants were not official delegates from the guilds, they could only discuss ideas to take back to their guilds for action. These representatives were from the Detroit Handweavers Guild, the Michigan Weavers Guild, the Greater Lansing Handweavers Guild, the Art Weavers Guild of Lansing, and Loomcrafters of East Lansing. The proposed organization would provide important educational and information benefits statewide; guilds were asked to approve the idea and send an official representative to the next meeting with the power to vote.

The first official meeting to organize the MLH was held on December 1, 1958, at Hartland. Beatrice Steyskal was elected chairman, and Ayliffe Ochs was made recording secretary—both to serve until a state meeting could be held and officers elected. Harriet Tidball agreed to act in an advisory capacity to the group. A temporary name, Permanent Conference of Michigan Handweavers, was to be used until a permanent name was adopted. Seven guild representatives attended: Steyskal, Ochs, Tidball, Dorothy Pfleiderer, Nell Sprinkle, Norrie Blakely, and Melvina McGarr (their guild names are not given in the records). The aims of the organization were "to help make available to all handweavers comprehensive knowledge and inspiration through the sponsorship of lectures, conferences, exhibits, source information, and other cooperative activities in the field of hand-weaving," and these aims were "to be accomplished through individual and group participation."[4]

Choosing a Name

On February 2, 1959, with the temperature at eighteen degrees below zero, the leaders and committee members met again in Hartland to decide on a name and to hone ideas for its first conference. Letters with comments from guilds around the state were read. The permanent name of Michigan League of Handweavers, suggested by Garnette Watters, past president of the Michigan Weavers Guild, was adopted. Much thought was given to the selection of a name. The committee felt that the word *league* suggested a "banding together." Ayliffe Ochs said, "It is our hope and our wish that all weavers in our State will come to cherish this name and that they will also contribute towards its greatness." Thus, with a name suited to their purpose, much enthusiasm, and only five months remaining for planning, the first conference for the fledgling MLH was discussed and set.[5]

Plans developed quickly for the group's first convention, at Walden-woods near Hartland on July 24–26, 1959. It was to feature exhibits of members' work, short talks and discussions, or a workshop. The committee needed to formulate details of membership and the structure of the organization. Those guilds that had sent in membership lists were asked to reserve four to fifteen places each at the convention, to guarantee sixty-nine attendees and thus sufficient funds. Joyce Jones and Ethna Brown of the Ann Arbor Guild were to chair the event. This first Michigan League of Handweavers conference attracted 135 weavers from Michigan, neighbor states, and Canada. Principal speakers included Osma Gallinger of Creative Crafts, East Berlin, Pennsylvania; Harriet Tidball, director of the Shuttle-Craft Guild; and Heather Thorpe, director of education for the University of Michigan's Museum of Natural History. Renowned weaver Dorothea Hulse of Los Angeles also spoke. A fashion show was conducted by Helen Hill, the first president of the MLH and an adult education teacher in the Detroit public schools. The conference aim was "to make handweaving groups and individual weavers of Michigan acquainted with each other: to point out the weaving resources within the state; to show what is available in weaving literature; to attempt to formulate a plan of learning or education which will comprehensively cover all the weaver's needs; and to point

The first formal board of the Michigan League of Handweavers. *Front row, from left*: Joyce Jones, Garnette Watters, Bea Styskal, Lela Gordan, and Helen Hill. *Back row, from left*: Harriet Tidball, Nell Sprinkle, Ayliffe Ochs, and Marjorie Michel. (Photo courtesy of the Michigan State University Museum.)

a way to achieving this education."[6] This conference was designated the Mary M. Atwater Memorial Conference, because Mrs. Atwater had participated in the first (1938) and many subsequent national conferences at Waldenwoods. The second MLH conference (1960) featured a full weekend of displays, instruction, lectures, and awards for work in several categories. The direction had been set.

Workshops and Conferences

From its founding, the MLH and its leadership were very active in the fiber community, and the organization was asked to participate in exhibitions and other activities that were rewarding to its members and the community at large. Helen Hill, its first president, in her 1960 year-end report to the MLH board and members, stated: "One of the outstanding achievements of the League was an exhibit of weaving at the Historical Museum, Detroit . . . In response to the request [of the museum], it resulted in 78 pieces, 50 of which were used."[7] Workshops and conferences offered excellent opportunities for weavers to be kept current about the newest trends and ideas, with well-respected teachers and rising stars. In 1965, for example, Harriet Tidball, conference coordinator, changed the conference format, offering special workshops after the conference. Held in Grand Rapids, the conference included an invitational exhibition of outstanding national weavers and was curated by Walter McBride; conference topics ranged from designing functional textiles by Tonya Rhodes of Ohio State University (who later taught at Western Michigan University) to a talk on inspiration from nature for textile design by Else Regensteiner, head of weaving at the School of the Art Institute of Chicago. There was great interest in Dwight Kirsch's experiments with color effects using dried or fresh flowers and leaves. Kirsch was artist-in-residence at the University of Iowa. Post-conferences were a workshop by Kirsch; a workshop in bag making by Trudy Emerson, costume designer and weaver from Coronado, California; and "Creative Stitchery" by Grand Rapids artist and teacher Lois McBride. Those that attended these special workshops had an additional treat. Workshop participants were invited, at the end of each of the three days, to a buffet supper at Mary Sayler's home in Grand Rapids, a box lunch picnic at Robert Sailors's Grand Rapids country home, and an informal dinner outdoors at Harriet Tidball's home west of Lansing.[8]

After some years, the MLH established a pattern of events: a biennial and juried fall exhibition of members' work in an art gallery, hosted by a local guild; workshop weekends in even-numbered years; and a larger summer conference with workshops, seminars, exhibits, a fashion show, commercial vendor exhibits, and a keynote lecture in odd-numbered years. These events attract two hundred to three hundred participants. Outstanding teachers in handweaving and fiber arts are brought to Michigan to benefit members statewide. Some serve as distinguished jurors, who evaluate members' work in the exhibits. This encourages high standards of craftsmanship and originality. Cash and weaving supplies are awarded to winning entries in fashion, fiber arts, and functional fiber work. Vendors bring an array of materials and equipment, not usually available locally. The educational purposes of the organization are well served, and the events offer opportunities to form friendships and develop leadership skills.

JoAnn Bachelder recalls her first MLH conference in Grand Rapids, which she attended with three women from her guild: "Well, I was just blown out of the water! It was such a fantastic experience. The three of them remained to take workshops, and of course, I hadn't signed up. I had to go home. And I really did not want to go home. I wanted to stay. So, I vowed right then and there that the next time MLH offered any workshops, I was going to be on the list to take a class. So, I took classes and workshops from MLH every year from the late seventies. And back then, they used to offer two workshops a year, one in spring and one in the fall. And I have taken classes from absolutely fabulous instructors and gotten a really wonderful

Attendees of the Michigan League of Handweavers conference at Hope College in
Holland, June 2001. (Photo by Andrea Anderson. Courtesy of Cathy McCarthy.)

weaving education by doing that. So, I owe that to MLH."[9] Bachelder re-
members many icons of the fiber arts movement who have taught in Michi-
gan at MLH events: Gerhardt Knodel, Ana Lisa Hedstrom, Ed Rossbach,
Katherine Westphal, Warren Seelig, Lenore Davis, Anne Wilson, Sylvia
Heyden, Diane Sheehan, Ann Sutton, Diane Itter, Cynthia Schira, Arlene
Fisch, Naomi Towner, Bhakti Ziek, Michael James, Theodore Hallman,
Leslie Voiers, Dini Moes, Helene Bress, Deborah Chandler, Alice Schlein,
and Helen Jarvis.

Michigan guilds and the MLH have been fortunate to attract and bring
nationally prominent teachers and artists to the state as program and
workshop leaders and keynote speakers. During the 1980s and 1990s, Anita
Luvera Mayer from the Seattle, Washington, region has frequently led
workshops and been keynote speaker at MLH conferences and workshops.
Mayer's specialty, design and embellishment of art clothing, attracts a wide
audience, and her classes are always filled. Nancy Lyon taught innovative
uses of the weave structure crackle. "California Rags," taught by Trudie
Roberts, was very popular. Heather Winslow specialized in colors and
trends for garments. Virginia West gave workshops in the construction of
garments from various woven lengths. Sharon Alderman has taught a variety of topics in designing good fabric for clothing and interiors. Nancy
Hoskins introduced the techniques of Coptic tapestry weaving. Jason
Collingwood, continuing in the tradition of his father, has taught structures and techniques in rug weaving; Randall Darwall inspired members
with pattern and color in his hand-dyed and woven silk scarves, as Karen

Selk has done with her workshop "Silken Kaleidoscope." Sheila O'Hara brought a wealth of ideas in "Multiple Warp Weaving." Textile surface treatments have been of particular interest. Madelyn van der Hoogt (current editor of *Handwoven*)—who has taught (and written about) many topics, including drafting—recently held a workshop entitled "Fabrics that Go Bump," focusing on differential shrinkage. Shibori on the loom dyeing has been taught by Catherine Ellis and by Kay Faulkner of Australia, both of whom came up with the technique almost at the same time. Japanese basketry and packaging techniques were taught by Nancy Moore Bess. Daryl Lancaster, *Handwoven*'s features editor and color forecaster, has given clothing construction classes and juried fashion shows.

Two Years of Planning

Planning and staging the MLH conference involves all the Michigan member guilds, which take on the tasks in about thirty committees. A conference chair, traditionally the MLH president, meets regularly with the treasurer and a board of appointed chairs—for registration, workshops, seminars, fashion, and site—to make policy and strategic decisions and to keep everyone informed of the planning progress over a period of two years. The summer workshops for the alternate years usually are coordinated by the vice president, with an appointed board to chair the major tasks: lining up exciting workshops, arranging for the conference site and housing, handling registration and publicity, and supervising the event. Records have been kept for about two decades, so the planners know which types of workshops fill quickly. The group still has its strongest base in weaving, and usually there are two or three weaving-oriented workshops; at least one in dyeing, clothing, design, or structure; and one or two in new techniques.

Selecting workshop teachers is not a science, but the MLH members have a long history of sharing information about teachers. Workshops are evaluated by the participants, whose opinions are also solicited for new teacher recommendations. The committees check with their guilds and fiber friends for the latest and best teachers, and the final selections are made at a board meeting where all the materials are reviewed and discussed. Several of the workshop teachers have given many workshops in Michigan and are highly sought after. Their classes always fill, but the planners are careful to avoid too frequent repetition of one class. The MLH is always on the lookout for the new, rising stars in the field. Exposure at an MLH workshop often leads to other teaching opportunities as the word spreads—even more rapidly now than earlier, with weavers' growing use of chat groups on the Internet.

Managing the larger conference exerts great demands on the president/ conference chair and the board. All the elements must work together: the conference mounts a two-day schedule of seminars, a juried fashion show with a banquet, juried exhibits of fiber art and functional fiber, a keynote speaker, an MLH board meeting, and the MLH annual meeting with election of officers, informal lunchtime conversation sessions, and guild or MLH exhibits. A budget must be made and approved, and contracts are signed with the host facility and all the workshop and seminar teachers and keynoter. An attractive and timely brochure must be produced, along with materials to be available for each registrant. It takes a cool head and a steady hand to keep track of all the details, and that job usually falls to the president, who has learned something about the process by heading the summer workshop as vice president in the previous year. Each of the board members and committee chairs has a notebook—developed over recent years—with the necessary forms, policies, timelines, and words of wisdom. Each of these individuals adds information from the current year and passes the notebook on through the president to the next chair. The system works, thanks to the goodwill and spirit of cooperation fostered by many years of successful guild participation—and possibly because MLH members love these events and do not want to give them up.

The conferences and workshops are where MLH members engage in continuing education in their craft. They get to sample all sorts of processes

Table decorations with the theme "Here on Huron," woven by the Northeast Michigan Weavers Guild from reeds and grasses gathered from the lakeshore, for a conference of the Michigan League of Handweavers, 2001. (Photo by Norma Ewart and Kati Meek. Courtesy of the Northeast Michigan Weavers Guild.)

and techniques to see what they are about. They can count on a solid group of weaving workshops with teachers that will help them hone their skills and grow. And they have fun. What could be better than to spend a weekend away from your family responsibilities, on a college campus in the summer, with a group of like-minded and engagingly creative folks? True friendships are formed here, often through taking classes together, serving on committees, or just sitting together at meals. Members look forward to seeing a wide array of fiber work in the galleries, on the runway, and on the backs of MLH members who are not shy about wearing their wearable art. Prizes are awarded two ribbons—one stays in the gallery, and the other is attached to the member's name tag. By closing time, people are eager to get on the road home, but they are already planning for next time.

Keeping in Touch

Communication, an early goal of the organization, continues to be primary. The MLH publishes a quarterly newsletter, a directory of members, a list of weaving teachers in the state, and a list of colleges and universities with instruction in weaving or fiber arts. The MLH has its own Web site (http://www.mlhguild.com), to promote more rapid access to fiber events in the state. The quarterly newsletter includes a swatch and instructions for weaving, dyeing, or spinning. Although many members use e-mail extensively for committee work and planning, the newsletter continues in the printed form and is sent by bulk mail, largely because members want the real swatch and not a color picture. A compact disk with a complete set of swatch pages for the period 1971–2000 (with instructions) was produced for the MLH by Margaret Windeknecht. Membership has grown to an average of five hundred individuals and thirty-four member guilds in Michigan, Indiana, Ohio, and Canada.[10] The member guilds elect guild representatives who are expected to attend the quarterly board meetings and participate in the decision making. They then bring back information about MLH activities to their guilds. Not all guild representatives are able to attend, but following each meeting, minutes and handouts are promptly mailed out to all representatives. The representatives have portable notice boards to take to their meetings, on which they can post new announcements and general membership information. Board meetings are open to any MLH member who wishes to attend. Also, any member is eligible to apply for a financial scholarship to attend a workshop or conference that will further their education in the craft.

Member guilds plan their own programs and may apply to the MLH for financial support—for example, to bring in outside speakers. For several years, the guilds in the Upper Peninsula have banded together to hold a fall gathering with speakers and activities. The MLH acts as a clearinghouse of information about Michigan workshop teachers and speakers who will travel to guild meetings to present their programs. For some years, this information was published in a booklet sent to each member guild's program chair, but now the information is available at the MLH Web site. Currently, there are twenty teachers listed, with programs ranging from basic weaving, spinning, dyeing, knitting, basketry, paper making, and beading to a diverse collection of specialties. Some of the programs and their teachers are "Basic Drafting," Pamela J. Arquette; "Altered Surfaces," JoAnn Bachelder; "Double Weave" and "Sock Knitting," Gisela Bosch; "Knitted Dolls" and "Needle Felting," Kathryn Carras; "Liturgical Weaving" and "Weaving with Wire," Millie Danielson; "Blankets and Rugs," Jochen Ditterich; "Seagrass Soft Sculpture," Judy A. Dominic; "Dollmaking" and "Surface Techniques," Jennifer Gould; "Designer Yarns," Sandra Griggs; "Quilt Dyeing" and "Silk Ribbon Embroidery," Marty Lawrence; "Textile Conservation," Dianne J. Little; "Tartans," Kati Reader Meek; "Primitive Rug Hooking," Kris Miller; "Plants to Paper," Karen Koykka O'Neal; "Dyeing Cotton," Susan Peters; "Spinning Angora," Holly J. Shaltz; "Knit Amulet Necklace," Pat Thompson; "An Artist's Journey toward Content," Sandy Webster; "Design and Weaving on a Hand Jacquard Loom," Pat Williams; "Theo Moorman Techniques" and "Creativity," Kathy Zasuwa.

A National Guild for Weavers

Attempts to bring weavers together from across the country had started as early as the 1930 Weaving Institutes at Penland, Kentucky. These were followed by Mary Atwater's summer camps starting in 1937 and the National Weaving Institutes at Waldenwoods near Hartland, Michigan, beginning in 1938. It would take until 1969 for talk to gain momentum to form a truly national organization of weavers. It happened at the North East Weavers Seminar in Amherst, Massachusetts, when the group was challenged by a leading weaver, Berta Frey, "to do something about it." By September, Garnette Johnson of Connecticut had started putting together a group of volunteers representing all parts of the country. They made contact with 125 of the nation's leaders in the weaving arts and became convinced that there was adequate interest in a national guild.[11] The Handweavers Guild of America (HGA) was formed, with a board of directors chaired by Johnson. A structure, goals, and a national magazine, *Shuttle Spindle and Dyepot (SS&D)*, were proposed. Johnson was editor in chief, assisted by her husband, who was a printer; she served as volunteer executive director of the HGA.

The magazine would join two others pioneering this field: *Handweaver and Craftsman* (1950) and *Craft Horizons* (1948). SS&D began with a membership of twelve hundred people who responded to five thousand invitations sent out by the group. The first issue of the SS&D quarterly was published in December 1969. The magazine announced two Michigan editors, both MLH charter members and well-respected weaving teachers, who would begin their columns in the second issue. The editor for "At Your Request," a question-and-answer column, was Mary Sayler of Grand Rapids. Joyce H. Jones of Ann Arbor was editor of "Dye Pot." Sayler and Jones were also HGA board members. Michigan weavers supported SS&D's first issue: Fred Wessels, founder of Kalamazoo Valley Weavers and first treasurer of the MLH, wrote saying that he would hand carve wooden reed hooks and send one to anyone who would send him a stamped self-addressed envelope. He later wrote in to say that he had a great response. Dorothy Buell of Chassell sent directions and a diagram for a Finnish-style sauna *piika* (bath cloth) designed by her guild members, "with the hope that other weavers will enjoy making and using it."[12] HGA organizers enlisted a volunteer board by working through the network of local guilds to write a constitution and bylaws and to establish working committees. The HGA's first biennial meeting was held in Detroit in June 1972, at its first national convergence, hosted by the MLH.[13]

Else Regensteiner, head of the weaving department at the School of the Art Institute of Chicago, summed up the philosophy and potential for the HGA in the spring 1970 issue of SS&D: "Weavers of many different concepts and tastes expect inspiration and incentive from a new organization, forgetting their differences in the pursuit of common goals. All will agree that their efforts must be directed towards the establishment of standards which are very high: excellent craftsmanship, artistic achievement, and a professional approach." She went on to discuss the two types of weaving groups at the time: the so-called traditional weavers and the art-oriented contemporary group: "There is room for both, for each has much to contribute to the other. Any organization must rely on its mature, experienced members to supply a solid foundation for growth. Many traditional weavers have an invaluable font of knowledge and are meticulous craftsmen; they have much to give, to tell, to teach." But Regensteiner warned against being set in one's ways. She urged weavers to remain open to new ideas and to the new works that have taken weaving into the fine arts. She predicted a "fruitful and stimulating exchange of philosophy and concepts" as long as both groups learned to appreciate and encourage each other. She believed that new students should learn what had gone before and build on that, carrying the craft into the future as they become the teachers and artists.[14]

The First Convergence: Detroit, 1972

In 1972, the HGA put on its first national convergence, hosted by the MLH. The planners expected two hundred attendees and were overjoyed and chal-

FASCINATION WITH FIBER

lenged when over three hundred showed up.[15] The MLH had been asked to organize the conference, and Mary Sayler of Grand Rapids and Elizabeth Clark of Kalamazoo were cochairs. Many other volunteers from the eighty-five-member MLH were involved. Gerhardt Knodel, the new director of the weaving department at Cranbrook Academy of Art, recalls the group of women from the MLH who met with him and requested his participation in planning the conference: "I worked with Verda [Elliott] and Mary Sayler and that whole fabulous group of women who decided to make something national . . . they wanted to conquer the world. And they had such vitality . . . They were just so much fun." Not only did Knodel offer Cranbrook as the site of the postconference workshops, but he organized and sponsored a challenging invitational exhibit of leading contemporary weavers to be held at the school. During the planning, he suggested calling the conference a "convergence." He told the Michigan weavers: "You can't do it in the old, traditional sense. You have got to complement it with another level." Speaking of the gap between artists and craftsmen, he said, "We blasted things open." He argued that the term *convergence* brought them all together. Knodel explains: "I had been invited to join the faculty at Cranbrook. This place has a noble history in terms of its development of new, contemporary functional textiles. But I want to kind of bridge this space—to people who maintain the history of textiles in a respectable way, because I personally respect that. I respect tradition. And with the new work, I believed in it one hundred per cent, but I could not guarantee what its future would be. Why can't the two work side by side?"[16]

The first HGA convergence ran from Thursday, June 8, until Sunday, June 11, 1972, at the Sheraton-Cadillac Hotel in Detroit. The top speakers at the conference assemblies and banquet were Peter Collingwood of England; Glen Kaufman, former director of the Cranbrook weaving program; Barbara Shawcraft, noted for fiber environments; and Roger Thomason, who made loom-formed garments. Two afternoons were devoted to thirty special-interest meetings held in two sessions, so that attendees might explore four different subjects. Major attractions were the invitational exhibit at Cranbrook, called *FABRIcation '72*, and commercial vendor exhibits, organized by Linton Davidson of Davidson's Old Mill Yarns in Eaton Rapids. Following the convention, nine workshops for about two hundred people were held at the Cranbrook community. They included "Basketry" by Joan Austin; "Resist Dyeing Techniques," by Jim Bassler; "Three-Dimensional Knotting," by Francoise Grossen; "Color and Design," by Gerhardt Knodel; "Textiles of the Past: Inspiration for Now," by Mary Jane Leland; "Wall Hangings and Other Woven Objects," by Theo Moorman; "Principles of Pattern," by Richard M. Proctor; "Open Doors: Our American Indian Heritage," by Mike Selig; and "Fabric Environments," by Barbara Shawcroft.[17]

A tubular woven loom-shaped suit in plain weave, designed, handwoven, and constructed by Roz Berlin, ca. 1970. (Photo courtesy of Roz Berlin.)

Wearable Art Takes a Bow

At the first HGA convergence, Michigan weaver Rosalind "Roz" Berlin presented a special-interest seminar on designing and weaving tubular loom-shaped garments—the new look in handwoven garments. Berlin was working primarily with natural materials—wool, silk, and linen—which she felt "adapt[ed] well to the earthy designs" that she preferred. In 1968, Harriet Tidball had featured Berlin's work in her twenty-fourth monograph, *Contemporary Costumes: Strictly Handwoven.*[18]

Berlin remembers her seminar, "I was absolutely amazed at the positive response to this innovative work and new approach to clothing . . . Anita [Luvera] Mayer was in the audience and had just started to weave. She was wowed by these new ideas. We formed an immediate friendship. After this seminar, I was invited to give workshops and lectures everywhere."[19] Mayer would go on to become a popular workshop teacher; a star in design,

A gray wool coat in double weave, designed, handwoven, and constructed by Roz Berlin, 1968. (Photo courtesy of Roz Berlin.)

weaving, and embellishment of wearables; and author of *Clothing from the Hands That Weave* (1984) and several other books. Barbara Wittenberg of Southfield, who graduated from Cranbrook in 1971, was also designing and creating garments shaped on the loom. In the mid-1970s, she wrote *Alternatives to a Fig Leaf* (1972), a book "about woven clothes" that offered a new way to weave, shape, and construct garments, a style that became popular in the 1970s and early 1980s.[20]

Other Michigan weavers who were speakers and seminar leaders at the first HGA convergence include Georgie Elyane Bick, Donna Botero, Ingrid Cole, Jane Hawkins, Urban Jupena, Robert Kidd, Gerhardt Knodel, and Doris Loftis. Knodel helped draw leading weavers and fiber artists in the field to the invitational exhibit, as well as bringing important conference speakers and workshop leaders. This set an example for years to come, both for the national convention and for the MLH, which continued attracting prominent fiber artists to its biennial workshops and conferences.

This first HGA convergence still brings forth great memories. Sandra "Sandi" Lummen of Grand Rapids said that Joyce Jones of the Ann Arbor guild brought her member-friends to Cranbrook to prepare all the looms for the Moorman workshop and that workshop participants stayed in the Cranbrook dorms. Marj Mink of Ann Arbor remembers attending the "terrific" workshop on color and design given by Gerhardt Knodel.[21]

A Grand Convergence

The MLH agreed to host the HGA convergence in Grand Rapids, Michigan, in the summer of 2006. In contrast to 1972, the HGA now has a small headquarters with a professional staff, in addition to elected fiber artist board members from across the nation. The headquarters is able to assume legal and financial responsibility and overall planning for the national meetings, but it still relies on local guilds or state associations of guilds, such as the MLH, for advice, support, volunteer staff, and local arrangements. The MLH members serving on the committee for the 2006 HGA convergence include: Pat Brown, Liz Cowdery, Cathy McCarthy, Loretta Oliver, Nancy Peck, Martha Reeves, Jack Taylor, and Marta Williams. A typical convergence will attract around two thousand participants and offers three days of about thirty preconference workshops, about thirty one-day studio sessions, tours, gallery walks, an array of about 180 seminar sessions with featured speakers over three days, a professionally staged fashion show, several juried shows of fiber art in various categories, plus a huge hall filled with about three hundred vendors offering all possible supplies and equipment in the field of fiber arts.

The HGA has also played a key leadership role in communicating news and market information to its far-flung membership. It has developed educational programs that encourage the highest standards of craftsmanship, through its Certificate of Excellence (COE) program for individual study in handweaving, dyeing, basket making, and spinning. Michigan's Karen Yackell and Debbi Cooper have earned HGA's COE designation. Cooper, specializing in dyeing techniques, was awarded her designation in 1998. Yackell received her designation in weaving in 1992, with the specialized study topic "Paralleling the Development of Navajo and Gobelins Tapestries." Yackell traveled to the Southwest to study Navajo weaving and to France to study Gobelin tapestry weaving. The HGA sponsors scholarships for students in undergraduate or graduate programs in the field of fiber arts and awards for outstanding exhibited works at juried shows across the country. Its journal, *Shuttle Spindle and Dyepot*, is a must-read for people in the field, with news, instructional and inspirational articles, book reviews, calendar listings, and advertising. The HGA Learning Exchange offers an opportunity for participants to weave or spin samples and ex-

Lady, a tapestry in wool by Karen Yackell, handwoven as part of the requirement for her Certificate of Excellence from the Handweavers Guild of America, 1992. (Photo by Pearl Yee Wong. Courtesy of the Michigan State University Museum.)

change work in a small group project. The "Teaching and Learning through Correspondence" program offers students an opportunity to mentor one-on-one with a well-known fiber artist. The HGA has an extensive Web site, offering a wide range of resources to fiber enthusiasts (http://www .weavespindye.org).

The Exhibition FASCINATION WITH FIBER

Since its beginning in 1959, the MLH has worked with other institutions in promoting weaving and fiber arts and bringing them to the public. One of its most ambitious undertakings has been the exhibition *Fascination with Fiber: Michigan's Handweaving Heritage*, a collaborative project of the MLH and the Michigan State University Museum, curated by Marie Gile. The exhibition opened at the museum in March 2004 and ran through December of that year. It surveyed handweaving and the development of guilds in Michigan and also included an exhibit of contemporary work (the MLH Thirteenth Biennial Fiber Show, juried by Sigrid Wortmann Weltge) and an invitational exhibit of works by Michigan faculty instructors in fiber arts. The exhibition, toured Michigan for two years and represents a major undertaking, with the involvement of many members and the museum staff. Guilds in the MLH were invited to weave a portion of a large fiber map of Michigan and assisted in the preparation of a photo album for each guild's history. The project has been enthusiastically received and has led to the creation of an archive for MLH history at the museum and to this book on Michigan's handweaving history.

Pictured on pages 118–20 are award-winning pieces from *The MLH Thirteenth Biennial Fiber Show* (juried exhibit) held at the MSU Museum from March 21, 2004, through December 30, 2004, which later toured for two years. There were six Merit Awards given: Gretchen Huggett, Mary Lou

Scarves and stoles on display in the *Fascination with Fiber* exhibit at the Michigan State University Museum, December 2004. (Photo by Pearl Yee Wong. Courtesy of the Michigan State University Museum.)

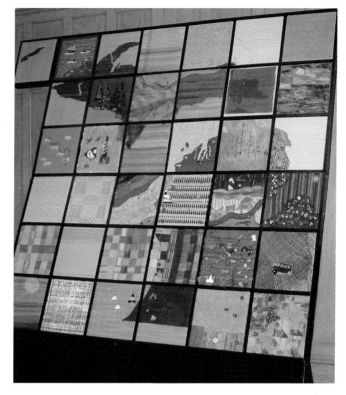

Great Lakes Gathering, a fiber map made by guilds from the Michigan League of Hand-weavers, on display during the *Fascination with Fiber* exhibit at the Michigan State University Museum, December 2004. (Photo by Marie Gile. Courtesy of Marie Gile.)

A view of the historic *Fascination with Fiber* exhibit at the Michigan State University Museum, April 2004. (Photo by Pearl Yee Wong. Courtesy of the Michigan State University Museum.)

Between the Rocks, a hand-dyed and woven wool wall hanging by JoAnn Bachelder, 2004. Awarded Best Fiber Art. (Photo by Pearl Yee Wong. Courtesy of the Michigan State University Museum.)

Illumination, a wall hanging of hand-dyed and woven silk, silk bouclé, and wool by Joanne Cromley, 2003. Awarded Second Place Fiber Art. (Photo by Pearl Yee Wong. Courtesy of the Michigan State University Museum.)

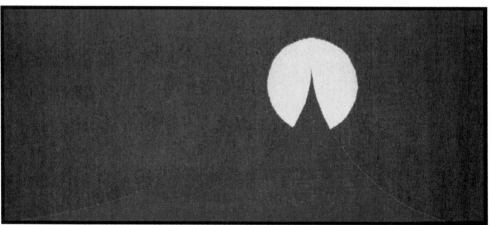

Splendid Table, a table runner and six place mats of linen, rayon, and washable spun paper by Elizabeth Leifer, 2004. Awarded Best Functional Fiber. (Photo by Pearl Yee Wong. Courtesy of the Michigan State University Museum.)

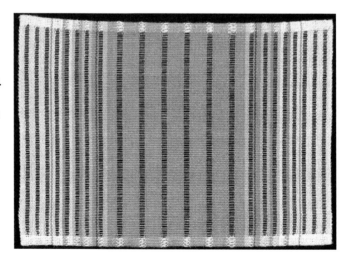

Scandinavia Remembered, a tapestry of wool on cotton by Millie Danielson, 2004. Awarded Third Place Fiber Art. (Photo by Pearl Yee Wong. Courtesy of the Michigan State University Museum.)

Detail of *Ritual Vestment*, a clerical stole of felted wool, layering, and beading by Laura Seligman, 2003. Awarded Second Place Functional Fiber. (Photo by Pearl Yee Wong. Courtesy of the Michigan State University Museum.)

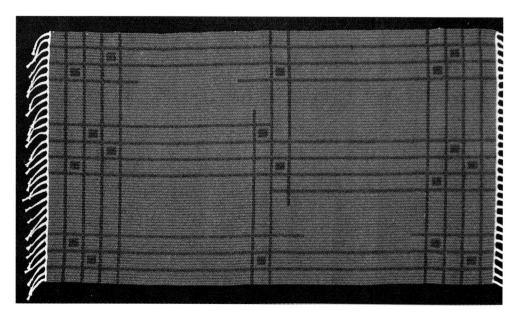

Lines and Squares, a rug constructed of wool on linen by Mimi Zoet Cummings, 2004. Awarded Third Place Functional Fiber. (Photo by Pearl Yee Wong. Courtesy of the Michigan State University Museum.)

Circus, a tapestry of wool on cotton by Priscilla Lynch, 2003. Awarded the Handweavers Guild of America Award. (Photo by Pearl Yee Wong. Courtesy of the Michigan State University Museum.)

Koval, Cathy McCarthy, Loretta Oliver, Sue Peters, and Margaret Windeknecht. Their works are not pictured.

Although styles, materials, and interests change over time, each decade and generation renews its interest in handweaving and the fascination with fiber. Individual guild members come to board meetings and suggest speakers or workshop teachers. The MLH provides its members with cutting-edge leaders in the field. The organization fosters communication and is stronger than any one guild, with its financial resources and volunteer corps of people. Through these means, it is able to bring to the entire state the wealth of talent in the world of fiber arts. This leadership and sustained tradition of bringing the best to the state keeps the MLH strong as an organization. Without this tradition and leadership, it could have faltered, as so many volunteer organizations have done in recent years. Early on, the Michigan guilds and the MLH were run by women and men with time to devote to the organizational work. That is still essentially true today. The traditions of the Michigan guilds and the MLH will be carried on by the next generation of members who absorb and appreciate the past heritage of their craft and organizations and apply their own talents to keeping this valuable tradition alive for the state.

NINE

Finnish Rag Rugs
Keeping the Tradition Alive

The practices of making rag rugs and patchwork quilts grew from the same roots—the need to make use of every scrap of precious material and to give it a new life. In the United States, the woven rag rug became popular in the depression-era 1930s and 1940s and never really disappeared. It enjoys a revival in the present era of recycling and uncarpeted wood floors. Fondness for these enduring and humble forms does not restrain contemporary weavers from buying new material and ripping or cutting it up to make pieced quilts, rag rugs, and cloth-strip clothing. Traditional rag rugs are made from used and worn clothing, which the weavers prefer for softness and muted colors.

The rag rug tradition in Scandinavia dates from the 1700s, so most of the earliest surviving pieces are only remnants. A mention of "tatter" weaving is found in a Swedish will in 1773, which is believed to refer to a rag coverlet.[1] The earliest preserved examples are from 1834. Woven rag mattress covers were used on beds along with pieced quilts and rya knotted-pile covers. In the mid-1800s, manor houses had rugs on the floors, but farmhouses and cottages of the poor traditionally had bare wooden floors, scrubbed weekly.

When the wood-pulp industry in the 1860s in Sweden began to replace rags with wood pulp for making paper, people no longer had a market for their old rags. At about the same time, the wood-burning stove replaced the fireplace. As the standard of living improved, rag rugs turned up in ordinary farmhouses. At first they were saved for special occasions or used only in the parlor or hall, but later they were put into everyday use. Some rag runners were laid close together to cover entire floors, while others were placed in parallel rows with the wood showing between.[2] Rag rugs had become a popular Swedish tradition by the twentieth century and were a tourist item late in that century. Finland was a part of Sweden until 1809 (when it was taken over by Russia until 1917), and the textile history of the

Washing rugs on a dock in Tampere, Finland, ca. 1990. (Photo courtesy of Yvonne R. Lockwood.)

two Scandinavian countries is similar. Both have handicraft preservation societies and extensive museum textile collections, and both share a reputation for distinctive contemporary design. Today, Finnish rag rugs are made in traditional and contemporary designs.

In Michigan, the tradition of rag rug weaving is carried on energetically by the descendants of Finnish immigrants, whose forefathers began to settle in the mining and lumber country in the Upper Peninsula as early as the 1860s. Finns later worked in Lower Michigan as lumbermen and farmers and in Detroit in the auto industry.[3] Contemporary weavers—including a good number of them working in the Finnish tradition—turn out handsome rugs, mats, and clothing using rags.

Inspired by their common interest in the folk traditions of handweaving, Yvonne Lockwood and Martha Brownscombe launched a research project to study this tradition when both worked at the Michigan State University Museum in East Lansing. The museum has a large textile collection plus weaving looms and equipment. They wondered who made these rag rugs and where. In 1985, Lockwood, a folklorist and curator, and Brownscombe, a weaving instructor in the Michigan State University Department of Human Environment and Design and a 4-H program specialist, used a seed grant to conduct a survey and produce an exhibit. In the process, they realized that the Finnish American weavers outnumbered all the other ethnic rag rug weavers in the state. The National Endowment for the Arts funded further research. Over the next decade, Lockwood and Brownscombe talked to over a hundred people. They collected samples for the museum and, most naturally, ended up with a good collection of their own. Lockwood continues the work they began, and about eighty weavers have been interviewed to date.[4]

Why do people like rag rugs? Hominess, usefulness, warmth, versatility, and cost are what most often attract rag rug owners. Michigan is a state with many farmhouses and summer cottages, where the rag rug is very much at home. But it is also found in city houses, especially in kitchens, playrooms, family rooms, bedrooms, porches, utility rooms, and basements. In the depression years of the 1930s, many American women were encouraged to supplement the family income by weaving rag rugs on inexpensive and sturdy looms being manufactured to meet the demand. The popular Union loom and other factory-made looms of metal and wood were bulky and certainly not beautiful, but they were less cumbersome than the traditional barn loom of the immigrants.[5] As the hard times passed and the United States was engaged in a booming wartime economy, many of these short-term rag weavers left their looms.

But something else was at work for the Finnish Americans. The rag rug and the rugged hand-hewn looms were locked into the culture the immigrants brought when they came to the country. The rugs were a necessity for working families that knew how to make the most of their resources, but they were also something wonderful to behold and to create. It was hard work to cut all those rags and spend days winding warps and threading as much as the loom could hold—ten, twenty, or more yards. Yet there was a great pleasure in bringing beauty out of piles of worn-out work clothes, housedresses, aprons, shirts, sheets, and towels. Weavers had the repeated pleasure of seeing clothing from their own families worked into a design

Country Spinners and Bridge Shuttlers guild member Silva Freeman demonstrates weaving a rag rug at an Upper Penninsula county fair. (Photo courtesy of the Country Spinners and Bridge Shuttlers.)

that evoked powerful memories. Family history could be told in rag rugs, as it is in patchwork quilts. As one weaver told the researchers, "When you make something out of what people discard, then, it's a treasure."

Finnish American traditions associated with the rag rugs are strong. According to tradition, only recycled fabrics are used. In fact, as one weaver told Lockwood, "Half the fun is in the hunt." Besides, worn, old rags give you softer, mellow colors, which is part of the appeal. The Finnish American weavers say that they follow the tradition—they use the patterns learned from their mother or grandmother or neighbor and only vary the colors and length. A good rag rug in Finnish American tradition must be firm and tight, able to stand rolled up on its end without sagging. The selvages must be straight, without loops. There must be no light showing through the weaving, and the surface must be smooth. Experimentation with shaggy and hairy surfaces and ends hanging out might be artful but are outside the tradition. Some of the younger Finnish American weavers do ignore tradition knowingly.

"A good rug needs a good loom," says one weaver in the study. That may be the most important ingredient of all. Often, the looms used by the traditional weavers were handmade by the immigrant community members and handed down through the generations. They follow traditional forms from Finland, using hand-cut timbers for the uprights and logs for the beams. One distinctive design, called the tree or root loom, has a C-shaped upright made from a tree that grew with that special curve. These old looms may have two or four harnesses and are counterbalanced. The loom bench may be separate or built into the frame. Originally, heddles were string, and most of the parts, including gear teeth for the tension bar, were carved from wood. A loom like this will occupy about six to seven cubic feet of space. Some of the Finnish American weavers manage to find room in their homes for them, but the looms are very often relegated to a summer kitchen, sauna, barn, or porch where there is more space.

When Lockwood and Brownscombe set out to find the rag rug weavers, they quickly learned that everyone in a small community knew who the weavers were and how to find them. But when the two researchers asked questions about the making of the rugs, the weavers were puzzled. Why would anyone be interested in talking about that? When the researchers began to ask about buying a rug, the mood changed. That is what was expected. While some weavers sell at fairs and bazaars, most sell out of their house—to friends and neighbors. Some keep a pile of rugs on a bench by the door, but it is rare to find a sign that reads "Rug Weaver" at the road. The researchers interviewed the weavers and photographed them in the context in which they worked—preparing rags and weaving—and with the rugs. They also coordinated several gatherings that weavers attended with a sample of their rugs for documentation. Here, the researchers wrote out answers to questions on forms developed for the survey. When the

Irene Vuorenmaa weaving a rag rug on her hundred-year-old Finnish American tree loom, 1988. (Photo courtesy of Yvonne R. Lockwood.)

researchers were invited to coffee and a sweet, they knew they were really welcome.

In the past, a weaver needing rags to be prepared held a rag-cutting bee; this was an all-day wintertime group activity. Friends and neighbors brought food, and the hostess fed them. Newcomers were instructed not to include zippers and buttons in the rag strips. In fact, the pile of zippers, buttons, ribbons, and linings are often recycled.

The rug weavers were not reluctant to talk about their rugs and their looms, but since they had learned informally and knew the terminology in Finnish, they were likely to refer to a "thingamajig" or "whirligig" in English—or to just point to the item. The average age of the weavers in the study was about sixty, but recently, more of the younger women are weaving. They begin today, as always, by learning from experienced weavers how to cut the rags.

Through this project, the researchers met many talented women who welcomed their return visits. One of them, Ellen Angman, lived near Calumet in a two-story house quite a distance from the road. During the winter, she skied along a marked path in very high snow to the mailbox for her mail and the packages of warp yarns she ordered. When her weaving teacher decided at age sixty that she was too old to weave, she gave Ellen her loom, and Ellen dragged it by wheelbarrow to her farmhouse. Ellen died in 2002 at age ninety-two, still weaving. Her weaving legacy has been carried on by a daughter, two granddaughters, and many great-grandchildren and nieces. Four generations of the Angman family demonstrated their skills at the Michigan State University Museum's American Folklife Festival. Until Ellen met the MSU team, she used white warps; then she tried a few color stripes and even wove place mats. But "white [warp] was the best and strongest," she told the researchers. Ellen was honored with a 1994 Michigan Heritage Award.

Anna Lassila, too, was a first-generation American of Finnish ancestry. Like so many young Finnish American women, she worked as a domestic servant in Chicago for many years, returning to the Upper Peninsula when she was needed at home. Then she married. She had four looms: two for rag rugs, one for place mats, and the other for fancy work. She occasionally attended meetings of weaving guilds and took classes for fancy work, although she was not a guild member. Anna was especially proud of her rag weaving, of which she said to the researchers, "This is how people know me." In 1987, she attended the Smithsonian Folklife Festival in Washington, DC, demonstrating at her loom. During the last decade of her life, local galleries carried her work. In 1993, Anna was honored with a Michigan Heritage Award. She died in 2001 at age ninety-one.

The rag rug weavers have always sold their work. They realize that some of their customers from the city buy up their rugs and resell them at much higher prices, but most are not bothered by this as long as they get their price. In the United States today, rag rugs can be found at just about any craft fair and in many gift shops. Some are imported, usually not from Scandinavia but from countries with lower wages and their own textile traditions. Some are handmade by other American weavers continuing the tradition. Rags have been used in weaving and for quilts and clothing in many cultures around the world. In Michigan, it is very special that this Finnish immigrant tradition has been so lovingly maintained and continued by Finnish Americans.

TEN

Weaving in Higher Education

The Arts and Crafts and Bauhaus philosophies had a significant influence in the craft education of weaving in Michigan, but the state's public universities in the early twentieth century also tended to view weaving as a useful skill in their programs of industrial arts, home economics, occupational therapy, and art education. Additionally, Michigan universities and teachers colleges were concerned about developing teachers in these programs. The evolution of courses in weaving, textile design, and fiber arts reflects this changing mix of influences.

Weaving or fiber arts have been offered at a dozen of Michigan's colleges and art schools: Central Michigan University, the College for Creative Studies, Cranbrook Academy of Art, Eastern Michigan University, Finlandia University, Grand Valley State University, Kendall College of Art and Design, Michigan State University (MSU), Siena Heights University, the University of Michigan, Wayne State University, and Western Michigan University. It continues today in all but four (Kendall, MSU, Siena Heights, and Western).[1] Each school's weaving/fiber history tells a slightly different story. Some schools moved their curricula along with the development of the field into fiber arts, but others, especially those that began with specific functional weaving goals, met declining interest and decreasing support. Their stories begin with the earliest schools that offered weaving in a craft orientation and moved toward the art school focus. The histories of Cranbrook Academy of Art and the College for Creative Studies have already been discussed in chapter 4.

Eastern Michigan University: Crafts, Shop, and Therapy

At Michigan State Normal College in Ypsilanti, weaving made its first appearance in the crafts shop for women, under the industrial arts curriculum, which began in 1901. The name of the Industrial Arts unit was changed to Industrial Education and Applied Arts in 1956, when the college became Eastern Michigan College—later to become Eastern Michigan University (EMU) in 1959. It was one of the first schools to expand its manual training in this way.[2] The weaving courses were for students in elementary education, occupational therapy, special and general education, pre-engineering, and technical training for industry. From the start, the arts and crafts classes were specialized for men and for women and included art metal, leatherwork, bookbinding, pottery, weaving, and printing.

During the 1940s and 1950s, EMU students in home economics and occupational therapy who wanted to study textiles took the arts and crafts course in industrial arts, which also offered a weaving course "on demand." From 1964 to 1970, the occupational therapy department offered its own course in therapeutic weaving, intended to help people with disabilities.[3] Although the class was no longer listed in the catalog after 1970, weaving was taught along with other crafts for therapeutic use for some time. The looms were disposed of in 2001. At least through the early 1980s, occupational therapists knew how to weave and could use weaving in therapy. By the late 1980s, practices began to change, and now weaving is no longer taught in these programs, says Dr. Elizabeth Francis-Connolly, chair of the occupational therapy department at EMU.[4] Earlier, therapists had many patients in rehabilitation for three to six months, and weaving was an option for keeping them active and interested. Due to changes in health care in the 1980s, therapists today see people who are more acutely ill, and they see them for very short time assessments, often in homes or residential care. Mental asylums in Michigan and other states were closed or vastly reduced, and therapists now make more home visits, to find meaningful activities patients can undertake where they live.

Weaving was being offered at EMU in 1968 by the art department. Its "Design in Materials" course, taught by Dorothy H. Lamming, often featured weaving. Lamming also taught design and painting at EMU from 1947 to 1976. She became interested in weaving in the last decade of her career at EMU and taught students to spin and dye yarn and to weave fabrics and wall hangings. In the 1960s, weaving was attracting attention in the art world, and Lamming paved the way for EMU's textiles curriculum to be designed by her successor.[5]

Computers Play a Part

"Design a fiber program for us," Pat Williams was told in 1976, when she accepted a position at EMU. It would be one of ten areas of concentration in the art department. Williams had started in painting at California College of Arts and Crafts (now California College of the Arts) in Oakland, where she saw the textile studio run by Guermonprez. Although she was not allowed in (she was a painting major, and at that time, the divisions were strictly maintained), she explored on her own through workshops and books. She liked the interplay of texture and color, and it was as if a light-bulb went on: "Discovering fibers is discovering a vocabulary you never knew existed. You just know if it's right for you."[6]

Indiana University was an important school for fibers, headed by Budd Stalnaker and Joan Sterrenburg. It was especially good in dyeing and for its art history courses that covered African, pre-Columbian Peruvian, and Oceanic cultures. Williams's portfolio was accepted there, and because she had the basics in weaving before arriving at Indiana, she focused on dyeing and surface design. Her summer research job there was to make over one thousand dye samples, and she created a reference that formed the basis for a course she introduced later at EMU.

When she arrived at EMU, Williams found a hodgepodge of donated looms and no designated space for studio work. Today there is a suite of rooms: a weaving studio, a dye lab, a dark room, a surface design studio, a computer area, and a lecture space. There had originally been a basic weaving class for undergraduates and two for graduate students. Today, "Introduction to Textiles" is a multipurpose course introducing students to woven and constructed textiles, surface design, and nonwoven construction. It is taken by students in art education, interior design, apparel merchandising, and theater, as well as by fine arts students. The intermediate classes explore weaving, surface design, dyeing, and other techniques in detail. A "New Tools for Textiles" class covers new chemical processes, digital printing, and computer-aided weaving. In addition to the standard four- and eight-shaft floor looms, EMU has a sixteen-shaft Macomber Air Dobby loom and a Norwegian TC-1 loom with 1,320 warp ends. EMU offers BFA, MFA (studio), and MA (studio) degrees, and many of the students become art teachers in elementary and secondary schools. Some teach in other college art departments and/or establish their own production studios.

Williams was early to realize the potential for the use of the computer in weaving and textile design. Since 1990, she has investigated computer programs and learned to design for weaving on Dobby and Jacquard looms. The school recently approved a certificate program in Jacquard weaving, a series of intensive workshops held mostly during spring and summer that are open to nondegree students. "You do need to know a lot about weave structures to make the best use of the Jacquard loom," she says, "but you can start out with plain weave, twill, satin, and two-shuttle weaves." Williams's own weavings illustrate the potential power and complexity that can be achieved on the Jacquard loom. "The field of fibers has mushroomed," Williams exclaims, adding, "During the 1960s, even though there was a lot of excitement in fibers, one person could still learn the basics of processes, history, and trends. It was easy to feel you knew the field. Now you can

Fossil 1, a wall hanging hand-woven on a Jacquard loom with four wefts and treated with lye (for shrinking) by Patricia Williams, Eastern Michigan University, 2004. (Photo by Pearl Yee Wong. Courtesy of the Michigan State University Museum.)

specialize in whole new areas that were just being thought of back then." Williams cites the examples of quilting, embroidery, surface design, art-to-wear clothing, basketry, felt making, papermaking, and dyeing.

In 1996, Williams developed the Dyers List on the Internet, which she continues to manage because she considers it very helpful in spreading ideas and sharing information: "Many people in fibers are working alone, and it helps to be able to consult others with similar interests and experiences." She has also started a list for JacqCAD Master software users and the Jacquard List for members of her Complex Weavers Jacquard Study Group, which she heads. Williams uses her research time to develop more expertise in Jacquard weaving, working at the Jacquard Center in North Carolina and at similar centers in Montreal and Quebec City. She also is developing a colors/weaves resource for Jacquard weavers, to be used as a reference tool at the North Carolina center and at EMU.

New Textile Research

Computers are important to the research of the Textiles Research and Training Institute (TRTI) in the College of Technology at EMU. The college was formed in 1980 but has roots back to the school's first programs in industrial arts and vocational education. Today, the focus is on science, research, and teaching EMU students, plus outreach programs and workshops for industry.

Julie Becker, who has a BFA in textiles and an MS with weaving and pattern-making concentrations from Bowling Green State University in Ohio, heads the TRTI. Her specialty is training in computer-aided design (CAD), using Gerber technology developed for the sewing goods industry and applicable to the automotive industry. Dr. Subhas Ghosh, a textile engineer who came to EMU in 2002, teaches in and coordinates the college's program in apparel, textile, and merchandising and directs several research projects. Cathryn Amidei, who recently completed her MFA in textiles at EMU, is the weaver and instructor working with the loom and teaches the TRTI's introductory course using weaving. Becker says that this team has a strong focus on textiles and that she plans to develop additional courses in the area. The unit gets research grants and trains staff from the automotive and furniture industry in the use and application of CAD software. They cooperate with Pat Williams and the art department in offering Jacquard and Adobe Photoshop workshops that are open to the public.[7]

In 2004, the TRTI received a sixteen-shaft computer Dobby loom from the estate of Geraldine Single, formerly of the Ann Arbor Fiberarts Guild. The loom is used for research projects and for the class in textile structures where Amidei introduces the language and concepts of weaving and characteristics of color in fiber/woven structures. She encourages her students to take art and fiber classes to build on this introduction. The big loom is a part of the course, and Amidei is working out structures on it in conjunction with the unit's research projects.[8] One of these projects is implanting optical sensors inside fabric to be used by the military. When the fabric is made into a jacket, for example, the sensors monitor stress and heat temperature. This technology is not only useful for the military but could also be useful for seniors living alone. One student is working on a project to improve the bulletproof vest. Another is working with fibers developed from corn—polylactic acid (PLA). Dr. Ghosh says that some of the yarns today are stronger than steel and could be used in building materials.[9]

Michigan State University: The Women's Course

A new program called "The Women's Course" was introduced in 1896 at Michigan State Agricultural College (today Michigan State University) in East Lansing. Beginning in 1928, weaving was taught in the program, by Miss Julia Tear. She included warping the loom, understanding patterns, and weaving original designs. The Women's Course was introduced to apply science to the daily labors of women and to "emancipate them from the tyranny of the kitchen and the nursery." The course was not intended to "unsex women"; rather, it was argued that science would give woman the same kind of help in the household "that has revolutionized the tasks of man in the workshop."[10] Abbott Hall was refitted exclusively to house the ladies. Special courses in domestic economy included study about the home, food, clothing, and emergencies (first aid). Students took domestic art classes in sewing, millinery, art needlework, and dressmaking. Textile analysis and identification was added in 1908, when the department was renamed Home Economics. Tear continued to teach textiles and weaving courses until her retirement in 1952. In the 1930s, the program for women moved from a focus on the home to merchandizing—working in clothing stores or designing for the textile industry—in order to expand careers for women with home economics degrees beyond teaching.[11] The unit was called the School of Home Economics, with its own building on campus in 1956.[12]

A Focus on Human Ecology

In keeping with the changes in society in 1972, MSU's School of Home Economics was redesigned as the College of Human Ecology.[13] The chief purpose of the new college was to serve the community nationwide by re-interpreting home economics away from the domestic model of cooking and sewing into a more sophisticated and broader structure of human ac-tivities related to the surrounding community and the world. The goal was "to improve the human condition for individuals and families in the com-plex American society of today."[14] The Department of Textiles, Clothing, and Related Arts became the Department of Human Environment and De-sign and included Joanne B. Eicher, a specialist on sociocultural aspects of clothing and African dress and textiles; Virginia Beauchamp, who taught computer-based information systems; Anna Creekmore, who taught cloth-ing construction and design and costume history; and Robert D. Bullard, whose area was color, form, and texture in interiors. Weaving continued to be taught, but courses emphasized textiles and clothing in terms of the human relationship to these as part of the human environment. Dr. Sally Helvenston currently serves as chair of the department. The college awards three degrees: a BS in apparel and textile design, an MA in apparel and de-sign, and a PhD in the design and management of the human environment.

The weaving instructor at MSU from 1964 to 1976 was Ronny (Grace) Martin, a noted weaver of transparencies and the author of *Approaching Design through Nature—the Quiet Joy* (1977). Martin was doing transparencies in linen before Theo Moorman wrote her book on the technique, but Martin used a plain-weave threading. She taught in Canada before coming to MSU, where she taught basic handweaving and textile design courses. The weaving course covered basic instruction in preparing the loom, weaving a sampler to learn all the loom and hand-manipulation techniques, and drafting and reading drafts. "We always worked in pairs in the weaving class," explains Martha Brownscombe, who later took over as the weaving teacher. Students completed a full-size throw in a wool plaid and learned finishing techniques for fabrics. Natural dyeing of fiber for a wall piece completed the series of projects for the course.[15] Martin grew up with a mother and grandmother who were always quilting or stitching, and her Norwegian father's sisters were weavers. She began weaving when she studied applied art at Iowa State University in Ames, Iowa, when she was twenty years old. After she left MSU, she continued to be active in weaving guilds wherever she and her husband lived, and at age eighty-eight, her favorite weaving is fine silk yard goods.[16]

Martin's textile design class focused on surface techniques with various dye materials, silk screening and repeat designs, embroidery, stenciling, and printing in order to produce yardage. Many of the design exercises were related to nature. "I really responded to this class; it was the best," says Brownscombe. Martin was "a great teacher who always made positive and supportive critiques of the student work," and the students would strive to meet her high standards. Each spring, Martin selected the best work from all six classes she had taught during the year and presented those in an art exhibition at the MSU student union. The exhibitions were staffed by the proud students and eagerly attended by the community. Each weaving class took a field trip to Davidson's Old Mill Yarn shop at Eaton Rapids, where the owner talked about producing the yarns and introduced various types of yarns. "It was one of the highlights of the class. We car-pooled and we always stopped at a special bakery for sweet rolls," says Brownscombe.[17] When Brownscombe took over the weaving class as an instructor in the 1980s, she maintained the standards and goals of her mentor and added some ideas of her own, such as making a garment or an accessory piece. The 1970s had energized students about ethnic and environmental issues, but students were still headed toward careers in textiles. Courses in the psychology of dress included such practical applications as ways to design the best protective clothing for firefighters and pesticide technicians, for example.

A project sponsored by Amoco introduced new yarns for student experimentation, and several of Brownscombe's students won in yardage competitions for interior design that were held annually in Chicago. It was an exciting era and a challenging one in colleges and universities faced with new student interests, a growing demand for computer training and application, and budget cuts for higher education. Martin had worked in a fully equipped and dedicated weaving and textile studio. Brownscombe had to haul looms out of storage and trundle them to an available classroom, and she often brought in extra equipment and materials from home.

The university was in a budget and space crunch in the 1980s, and by 1994, the looms were loaned to a community program, with the intent of keeping the looms active and in working order.

A new era in computer-aided design began at MSU in 1988, with a large donation of textile design software from Computer Design Incorporated (now Lectra), originally based in Grand Rapids. This development contributed to a new focus on textile design that emphasizes knit, woven, and printed surface design, all developed on the computer. This focus on design technology reinvigorated MSU's program in apparel and textile design, and student enrollment in the program has rapidly increased. The latest addition to the program includes a digital fabric printer that allows students to print short runs of their designs for construction into apparel prototypes. "Currently, a new interdisciplinary design initiative has begun as the university undergoes reorganization. This should lead to greater opportunities for expanding the textile design portion of the apparel and textile design major, including reinstating the weaving program," says Dr. Helvenston, who hopes to set up a permanent weaving studio with the recently returned looms from the local arts group.[18]

Western Michigan University

Western Michigan University (WMU) in Kalamazoo offered weaving classes through its occupational therapy program, which began in 1922, but it is not clear when the first weaving classes began. They were available to undergraduates and graduates in the 1950s and 1960s. Training in crafts for occupational therapy was emphasized at least until Marion R. Spear and Jane Thomas retired. "Some older OTs still love the loom and the value it has in treatment," says Richard Cooper, a professor in the department, who adds that "no schools teach it anymore." Cooper, who is a weaver and a spinner, maintains: "The weaving process (including setting up the loom) has many aspects of cognition, problem solving, reach, strength, endurance, positive outcomes, organization, tenacity, and others that many clients need to work on. Weaving was a valuable treatment tool for people with strokes, spinal cord injuries, Parkinson's disease, traumatic brain injury, dementia, and others. The loom could be used for psychiatric treatment and with kids in schools." Cooper points out that weaving therapy lost favor as the treatment changed and that space, cost, and upkeep were all issues. But he notes hopefully: "There is movement in healthcare and reimbursement that is returning to functional outcomes and longer term care—and art/craft activities for home bound, homecare clients. The role that weaving may play again is not developed, but might see a comeback." Cooper's research includes work on the role of creative activity in human development, function, and rehabilitation. He works with artists and art therapists on a program developed for normal and dysfunctional groups.[19]

Weaving was introduced in the fine arts program at WMU when Helmi Moulton joined the faculty in 1960, and it continued until her retirement in 1988. Moulton had returned to college at Central Michigan University in 1956 after raising her children. She had intended to major in painting. Even though her mother wove in the kitchen on a big hand-hewn barn loom, Moulton had not been drawn to weaving in college. But one day, on an impulse, she signed up for the last place remaining in Professor Ux's weaving class. She says, "That was it." After that, she concentrated on fiber art, and she received her BS in 1960. While teaching at WMU, she commuted in the evenings to complete her MFA at Wayne State University.[20] Moulton offered beginning and advanced classes in textile design, supervising sixty students (most were undergraduates, but there were a few MFA students) in weaving, macramé, knitting, rug hooking, stitchery, quilting, silk screening, and spinning. Twenty-six floor looms and several table looms filled the textile studio at school, and Moulton worked on three floor looms during evenings at home. Her work ranged from large wall hangings to doll-like soft sculptures. She constantly collected fibers and natural objects to incorporate in her fiber art. She also taught weaving at the Grand Rapids Art Museum and at the Kalamazoo Institute of Arts. She was a popular teacher. One of her MFA students, Eve Reid, is currently an adjunct professor in the art department at WMU.

The focus was on weaving as an art, says Reid, but Moulton also demonstrated off-loom techniques. She encouraged students, including Reid, to supplement their studies with "very valuable workshops offered by the Michigan League of Handweavers and the Kalamazoo Handweavers Guild, which brought in all the latest teachers and techniques."[21] Reid currently teaches papermaking and includes fiber techniques in her art education classes. She also has taught at the Grand Rapids Art Museum and at the Kalamazoo Institute of Art. WMU's art department stopped teaching weaving after Moulton retired. WMU sold the looms and used the space for a new computer lab.

Fibers in the Art Departments

The 1970s were the golden age for weaving in higher education in Michigan. Six artists assumed direction of new or reorganized fiber programs in the art departments of institutions of higher learning during this time: Gerhardt Knodel at Cranbrook Academy of Art, Sherri Smith at the University of Michigan, Pat Williams at Eastern Michigan University, Urban Jupena at Wayne State University, Susan Aaron-Taylor at the College for Creative

Studies, and Elizabeth Leifer at Finlandia University. They came from art schools in California, Indiana, Kansas, Pennsylvania, and Michigan, bringing fresh points of view and energy to a growing field of fiber arts. They developed curricula and expanded the range of study to include dyeing, surface design, paper, mixed media, and computer applications.

Wayne State University

Wayne University (later Wayne State University [WSU]) in downtown Detroit first offered courses in textiles and weaving in 1933, in the College of Education. The first weaving class was held on the Cranbrook Academy of Art campus and was taught by the Swedish weavers in Loja Saarinen's studio. In 1936, the class in weaving textiles was placed in the Department of Art and Art History. Nellie S. Johnson, who started teaching "Creative Weaving" for Home Economics in 1937, was moved to the art department in 1939 to teach the weaving class and a textile art history course. When Johnson died in 1952, Ruth Ingvarson, who had established a studio in downtown Detroit, took over the classes from 1952 to 1968. Eleen Auvil, a 1961 MFA graduate from Cranbrook Academy of Art, was hired in 1968 to head the weaving department. Her plans were to develop a complete fabric design and weaving course in conjunction with the art department's degree program in crafts. Auvil had a studio in Romeo, Michigan, where she designed rugs, pillows, tapestries, and wall hangings.[22] When she moved away in 1972, Urban Jupena, another recent Cranbrook graduate, was hired to teach fibers.

When Jupena arrived, the art department's focus was on fine arts—drawing, painting, and sculpture—with design taking a lesser role. Currently, the focus is still on fine arts, but students in this urban center need to graduate with real-world skills that help them get jobs. Today, the majority of art students are in fashion design and interior design. WSU is the only Michigan art school offering fashion design, and Jupena has geared his program to give design students something special for their portfolios. In addition to courses teaching them how to design, sew, drape, and alter patterns, the students take fiber courses that teach them how to make their own fabrics, either woven or with surface design and embellishment. With this knowledge, they can create "completely unique" pieces.[23] The fashion department requires students to take weaving and surface design courses, and this has kept the fiber department healthy. As is the case in many schools, the fiber program is small, but looms take studio space. WSU has twenty looms for beginning students and five large Bexell/Cranbrook looms for advanced students, and the school has plans for obtaining an AVL computer loom. "Trends come and go," Jupena notes, but computers are pervasive

Sibyl, a wall hanging of cut woven flossa by Urban R. Jupena, Wayne State University, 2004. (Photo by Pearl Yee Wong. Courtesy of the Michigan State University Museum.)

today. He explains: "We are in the fine arts department, not a technical school. We expect technique to become so natural for students that it falls away when they create the soul of a piece."[24] Some students are already entering his program with experience in using the computer for design, but they often lack artistic ability and an understanding of fiber structure. WSU offers BA, MA, and MFA degrees in fine arts, and a student may focus on weaving or surface design but will have experience in both. Each graduate student applies with a portfolio that is evaluated by a faculty committee from the art department, and Jupena is the adviser for the fiber arts program. He establishes a six-member committee of faculty to work with and evaluate the student's graduate work.

Jupena's own work focuses on the creation of interior pieces for homes and offices, including sculpted fringe rugs and decorative screens, wall hangings, and textile prints. In 1987, he reorganized the Michigan Surface Design Association, affiliated with the national Surface Design Association. "At that time," he said, "there was no real state organization that dealt with fiber students who were not weavers." The weavers' guilds were open to fiber arts, but this group would focus on learning and exploring new techniques for surfaces of all types. Many in the group are his former students and enjoy the opportunity to keep growing. They hold workshops, lectures, and juried shows.

Central Michigan University

At Central Michigan University (CMU) in Mount Pleasant and at the University of Michigan in Ann Arbor, weaving has always been in the fine arts schools, but art education was the early focus. Katherine Ux came to CMU in 1944 with a BA degree from Western Michigan University and an MA from Columbia University. Ux had first taught painting at Alma College, and during the 1940s and 1950s, she taught courses in textiles and textile design, along with other fine arts courses, at CMU. Her first textile courses covered the study of textile composition and included basic instruction in weaving.[25]

In 1960, Ux designed new courses and offered two sections of the class "Weaving as a Creative Art Form." She credited her study of weaving in the art school in Stockholm, Sweden, in 1955 as a major influence in designing the new courses. Although she had first taught painting, once Ux learned to weave in Sweden, she excelled in her new medium, and her works were sought after. Ux was "ahead of her time with innovative, avant-garde art," says Bernice Sizemore, one of her students, who adds, "She inspired and introduced thousands of CMU students to the intricacies of weaving."[26] Her CMU students were to meet three hours a week, whereas the Stockholm class had met all day for six days a week. Ux's challenge was to cram so much into a short time period and also inspire students to be creative. She came up with a scheme that she shared with other weavers in *Handweaver and Craftsman*.[27] In the first part of the class, each student would set up a different structure on each loom, with enough yardage to allow every student to work all the looms (a round-robin approach). The students moved from loom to loom and experimented with all sorts of yarns, discovering variations and developing ideas for their own, unique projects for the second part of the class. Ux was delighted with the results. When she retired in 1975, there was a series of replacement teachers—Mildred Hines (1976–77), Valerie Dearing (1978–79), and Diane Deyo (1980–81)—until the school hired Sally Rose to lead the department.

Papermaking: A New Focus

Teachers heading Michigan's programs in the fiber arts frequently find themselves teaching all the processes plus some fiber history, because the programs are quite small. Each teacher has strengths in one aspect of the field and can usually manage to find lecturers or advanced graduate students to help teach other aspects. At CMU, Sally Rose, who has headed the fiber program since 1983, creates designs for vessels or sculpture from soluble paper bonded to sticks and other natural objects. Rose has the most advanced papermaking lab in the state. At EMU, Pat Williams is an expert

Pretty Is . . . , a wall hanging of handmade paper and stitchery by Sally Rose, Central Michigan University, 2004. (Photo by Pearl Yee Wong. Courtesy of the Michigan State University Museum.)

in computer-loom skills. Rose and Williams have exchanged workshops for their students, with Williams giving demonstrations on CMU's computer loom and Rose taking her papermaking process to EMU for a workshop.

Rose, who first learned weaving at Colorado State University from Warren Seelig (a CAA graduate), became interested in paper when she studied at Indiana University and was the student assistant to Joan Sterrenburg, who worked in surface design and paper. At CMU in 1983, Rose inherited a program of courses ranging from introductory textile design and weaving as a creative art form to intermediate and upper-level studio courses. Rose developed a broader spectrum of fiber courses, so that all students have a good, solid background in loom work, tapestry, and off-loom techniques and processes, including dyeing, basketry, felting, and fabric collage. The curriculum now includes distinct courses in surface design and papermaking. CMU's program offers BFA, MA, and MFA degrees. It attracts students from other departments and has become more sculptural—with anything you can call "fiberous" being fair game to use in making a visual communication. Rose explains: "What the art departments are trying to do is different from what the weaving guilds do. We pay attention to craft and appropriate materials, but the concepts or impetus for making a fiber piece are different from what will look effective on the dining room table, or what drapes and wears well for a hand woven garment." Rose appreciates having a strong guild system in Michigan, because "a lot of the truly technical information about weaving in particular is being preserved by the membership of the weaving guilds." She takes her students to fiber-art exhibits sponsored by the guilds, to help develop their sense of the field and its history and traditions.[28]

The University of Michigan

Although the University of Michigan offered weaving as one of the skills in its art education program in the 1960s, fibers did not become a concentration until 1974. Wendell Heers and Julia Andrews taught the secondary art education classes, which included weaving and metal jewelry work. Heers specialized in jewelry. He was not a weaver, but he directed students who experimented with designs on the tapestry loom: "They did some wonderful work. Fibers and fabrics are such an important part of our lives from birth onwards that they just had a feel for it."[29] Like most other art schools, the University of Michigan followed the Bauhaus method for teaching art, with a grounding in the visual arts—basic drawing, figurative (life) drawing, two- and three-dimensional design, and color theory—before moving into specialized areas. Teachers of the education classes were hired as producing artists and were tenured in art, just like all the rest of the faculty. "The U of M thought of the crafts as an extension of the fine arts," Heers said. In the 1970s, the crafts movement was really strong, and Michigan brought in artists with international reputations to head areas of study in fiber, metals, and ceramics. In 1974, the art department moved into its own new building on the North Campus, with facilities specifically designed for the new units.

Sherri Smith had a dream assignment in 1974—to come to the University of Michigan, develop a program, and outfit a new lab. She had completed her studies at Cranbrook Academy of Art and was teaching at Colorado State University. Michigan interested her as a great place to live. Her goal for the program was to cover the whole fiber field—weaving, surface design, and off-loom fiber structures. She has since given the undergraduates a wide exposure to the field and worked individually with graduate students, helping them develop an area of interest and filling holes in their knowledge.[30] She has a large weaving studio, with eight- and

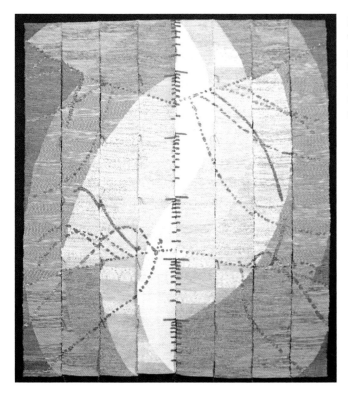

Parameters for the Higgs Boson, a wall hanging woven with cloth strips by Sherri Smith, the University of Michigan, 2004. (Photo by Pearl Yee Wong. Courtesy of the Michigan State University Museum.)

sixteen-shaft floor looms for the advanced students and smaller, four-shaft looms for the introduction sessions. The surface design lab is equipped with work tables, commercial sinks, burners, draining racks, and dye storage. A smaller room houses sewing machines.

Until the fall of 2003, undergraduate and graduate students were admitted to the university's School of Art and Design and could concentrate in fiber. Graduate students were admitted in special fields, one of which was fiber. Earlier in the university's program, the students took the standard Bauhaus foundation courses, but more recently, the foundation courses were assigned to the divisional fields. Now, with a new dean and a new unified program, all undergraduates in the first two years take a broad introduction to media and ideas, including courses in materials, processes, drawing, and computer design. After that, each student develops an integrative final-year project to earn the BFA in Art and Design. The new MFA in Art and Design, begun in 2003, requires three years of work, with an in-depth connection to a field of study outside art and design. In the area of fiber, the new program means that Smith and a team of instructors teach sewing skills and shibori dyeing in seven-week sessions. Smith reports, "The students are very happy about it—men and women—being able to sew and mix dye colors." She keeps a loom set up in the sewing studio, where students are welcome to experiment, but mostly they are too busy. She hopes that their interest will be stimulated and that they will enroll in her junior-level introductory course in the fiber arts, where they will weave and do surface design. "The old program encouraged narrowness and made it difficult for students to transfer into new-found areas of interest," says Smith, adding, "This one encourages experimentation and broadening of one's knowledge."[31]

Smith's students may go into teaching, studio art, or design for the textile industry. She works to give them a strong foundation for whatever direction they may choose: "Art school gives students the vocabulary and formal concepts so that they can talk about art. It teaches general skills, composition and color use, how to mix colors, and sets up patterns of thinking and experimenting." Smith explains: "We hope to make them more ambitious artistically. The first sketch or drawing you do is not likely to be the best or ultimate choice. We want them to know that the chances are that you can improve."[32] Smith hopes that the education the students receive develops those patterns and insights. Smith worked as a designer of textiles before teaching, but she is most noted for her early sculptural weavings and her contemporary wall hangings, which often reflect a fascination with mathematical sequences.

Finlandia University in the Upper Peninsula

Suomi College at Hancock became Finlandia University in 2000. It was founded in 1896 by Finnish immigrants as a small liberal arts college on the Keweenaw Peninsula, serving the sister cities of Hancock and Houghton. When Elizabeth Leifer joined its art department in 1976, she had been working for several years as a designer and color consultant for architects and engineers on schools, hotels, and hospitals. She received her BA in painting and design in her home country of Australia and her MFA in design and color at the University of Kansas. Suomi College had offered a weaving class in the year before her arrival, so she found the classroom equipped with rigid heddle looms for thirty-six students. Leifer focused on structure and color in her first classes and quickly set about developing a fiber concentration and securing four-shaft looms.[33]

In 1996, fiber and textiles were included in the school's Suomi International College of Art and Design, which offered four-year BFA programs in fibers, ceramics, and industrial design. The focus was more on design than on fine art. Classes were career-oriented. All of the students took art foundation classes and also worked in another artistic process beyond their major. Leifer's fiber courses covered weaving structure, fiber development and history, art and industrial applications, surface design, dyeing techniques, shibori, *devore* (surface etching), and other resist and photographic methods. She added a dye studio and, in 1997, obtained a sixteen-shaft AVL loom. (Currently, they have a twenty-four shaft AVL Compu-Dobby loom.) Students held off-campus internships and presented their work in the senior year. Leifer calls her own technique "painting in a woven structure." An example of this technique is her piece in the entrance lobby of Marquette General Hospital, in which the northern lights dance across a graded-color background.

When Leifer retired in 1999, Phyllis Fredendall, who began teaching at Finlandia in 1993 as an adjunct faculty member, took over the fiber program. Fredendall completed her BFA in fiber in 1990 at Northern Michigan University and is enrolled in the MFA program in interdisciplinary art at Goddard College in Vermont. Fredendall added more off-loom techniques, including felting, knotting, and wrapping. Currently, one-tenth of all art and design majors at Finlandia are fiber majors. Some students are interested in teaching and gallery work; others hope to go into designing for industry. They take core art and design courses; two business courses; and classes in on- and off-loom weaving, fashion design, and surface design. These students are encouraged to take a semester abroad at the sister school, Kuopio Academy of Design in Finland, which has large departments in weaving, printing, dyeing, and garment design.

Fredendall grew up in the Upper Peninsula and says that she has been influenced by the traditions of the rag rug weavers. Her own weaving has changed and evolved. She uses the loom "as a sculptural tool, creating deep relief and free standing sculpture." But she is also interested in functional work, carpets, and cloth for garments. Fredendall says: "I love to weave. It connects me to my past and other cultures."[34] She has concentrated on felt making for the last three years and is "developing memory maps as a vehicle for personal narrative."[35]

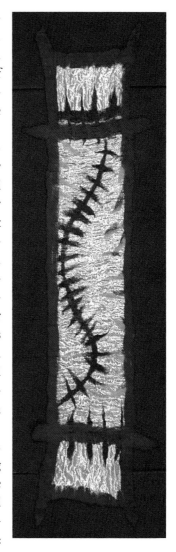

Railway Track Memory Map: Now and Then, a felted wall hanging by Phyllis Fredendall, Finlandia University, 2004. (Photo by Pearl Yee Wong. Courtesy of the Michigan State University Museum.)

Siena Heights University

Weaving was taught in the art department at Siena Heights University in Adrian by Sister Jean Agnes Klemm, OP, from 1970 to 1991. She had been teaching English to Spanish-speaking children in Puerto Rico when she was summoned by her natural sister, Sister Jeanine Klemm. Sister Jeanine had a PhD in art—with metalwork and calligraphy as her specialization—from Columbia University in New York City, and she headed the art department at Siena. She needed a weaving teacher. Sister Jean Agnes says she learned weaving on the job, but she enjoys the work so much that, at eighty-six, she continues to weave things for the school's gift shop and for friends. In 1991, when Sister Jeanine died, Sister Jean Agnes stopped teaching, and the weaving program ended.[36]

Kendall College of Art and Design

Weaving was included in the interior design program at Kendall College of Art and Design in Grand Rapids for about a decade, starting in 1982. Sandi Lummen, who had studied at Indiana University, finished an MFA in art/fiber at Western Michigan University in 1983, under Helmi Moulton's supervision. Kendall hired Lummen just as the Grand Rapids Art Museum was closing its extension weaving course. Kendall College bought the looms, and Lummen developed the college's weaving course. A decade later, Kendall developed space problems, so weaving and the looms had to go. Lummen returned to her first love, painting, and continued to teach foundation courses in the fine arts department until 1992. Her undergraduate weaving classes were always filled, but she thinks that weaving works best as a graduate program, because it takes so much time to develop the technical and artistic skill to do it well.[37]

The Grand Rapids Art Museum, under the direction of Walter McBride (1954–70), had introduced art classes for college credit and noncredit. After an informal arrangement involving Western Michigan University, the University of Michigan, and Grand Valley State University, the museum worked with the University of Michigan's Grand Rapids Regional Center to offer extension credit classes. Weaving classes began in 1948 and ran until 1981, when the University of Michigan's extension office closed and the museum planned to move.[38]

Grand Valley State University

Although some fiber programs were closed by the end of the century, a new one began. At Grand Valley State University, a new class was offered in the winter of 2004. Professor Ann Baddeley Keister, a tapestry artist, first taught the fiber class. She also teaches two-dimensional design, as well as color and design, in the art department at Grand Valley State University near Grand Rapids. Her class in surface design covered painting, stamping, printing off the computer onto fabric, piecing, stitching, beading, and other surface embellishment. Keister has a BFA and an MFA from the University of Kansas and taught at Kansas and Indiana universities before coming to Michigan. Her work appears in *Fiberarts Design Book 5* and *Fiberarts Design Book 6*.

Fiber Education

Students in Michigan in the twenty-first century have a rich selection of courses in fiber education, both undergraduate and graduate, from which to choose. The programs have different approaches and strengths. Most of the faculty members have been in place for a couple of decades and have honed their expertise in their art and teaching. All exhibit their work in Michigan and at various galleries and museums across the country. But this century will bring replacements and change. In fact, changes are already evident. The University of Michigan has revamped its art curriculum to make it more flexible and has redefined the foundation courses, retaining drawing and including computers and digital design. Central Michigan University has returned to offering a required foundation core for all its art students. Eastern Michigan University is offering a certificate program in Jacquard weaving. Most of the programs have at least one computer-aided loom and are teaching the most recent and exciting techniques in surface design. Cranbrook Academy of Art dropped its emphasis on designing for interiors and industry, and weaving has become one technique among many taught at Cranbrook, where the emphasis is on cutting-edge art. Michigan State has developed a new program in textile design using computers and digital printers. The shift to fiber programs reflects this field in higher education nationwide: a few schools are specializing in design for industry, but most are treating fiber as an art, albeit one recently arrived at this new status. A good portion of the basic instruction available in handweaving, spinning, and (to a lesser extent) dyeing is left to the community arts centers and the weaving and fiber arts guilds and their workshops.

ELEVEN

Conclusion

Weaving has changed significantly since Michigan's early years, moving from a craft of necessity to a recreational activity, involving the support of a guild or group, or to a professional career in teaching or studio art. Looking back over modern-era changes, Irene Waller, in her book *Textile Sculpture*, points to the early twentieth century Arts and Crafts movement, the Bauhaus movement and the upsurge of fiber art activity in Eastern Europe, and the important museum exhibits in Western Europe (such as the International Biennials in Lausanne, Switzerland, and the Museum of Contemporary Crafts and the American Craftsmen's Council shows in New York City) as major influences toward these changes. Waller says that these institutions and events have "shown the world what was happening" in weaving and fiber arts. "From there on," she explains, "the movement has spread ever further and the use of fiber, thread, and textile-based methods of construction as an art medium is now a fully-recognized and world-wide movement."[1]

Since World War II, the world has become interconnected, global. New ideas and images sweep back and forth with the touch of a computer stroke. People continents apart link up through the Internet to discuss ideas about weaving, fiber arts, and surface design. The pendulum swings between artistic focuses. Tapestry is once again of interest, but it is no longer confined to a traditional rectangle or flat surface. Sculpture, mixed media, urban forged pieces, installations, and video and digital art have swept into fashion. Ikat and shibori dyeing and holes, bumps, and pleats create new surface interest. Yardage is also back, offering great swaths of new fibers in new and familiar materials, many with digital imaging and computerized Jacquard compositions. The increasing array of resources is exciting and open to artists, designers, professional and recreational weavers, and hobbyists.

Today, ample opportunities for study beyond formal higher education abound for weavers and fiber artists at all levels, including national conferences, such as the HGA's convergence and the Surface Design Association's conference; classes at schools, such as Penland School of Crafts,

Arrowmont School of Arts and Crafts, Haystack Mountain School of Crafts, and others; and workshops, seminars, and lectures available through guilds and other organizations. In Michigan, the Michigan League of Handweavers and the Michigan Surface Design Association offer a regular program of workshops, conferences, exhibits, and juried shows. The new Michigan-based Fiber Arts Network (FAN) serves as a channel for information within the state about fiber activities and also sponsors juried exhibits. Books and magazines (*Handwoven, Shuttle Spindle and Dyepot, American Craft, Fiberarts, Surface Design*, and *Textile Forum*—the last from Europe, in English) are there to inspire, alongside local and traveling exhibitions. Some weavers will quickly adapt to the computer and computer-aided looms and eagerly explore new techniques for creating beautiful and useful objects, expressing emotions, and conveying ideas; others will always prefer the traditional tools and patterns for these purposes. Outdoor craft fairs, handicraft workshops, and informal education in the fiber arts offer new opportunities to explore a wide range of techniques. In the recent past, some of the weaving guilds opened their doors to the total range of fiber arts—surface design, computer and digital art, beads, baskets, metals, and quilting—and found growing interest, new members, and an influx of new ideas. Some changed from weaving to fiber arts guilds, a big step for many. The Michigan League of Handweavers and the Handweavers Guild of America are today much broader in their interests than their names suggest. Their conferences, exhibitions, and publications cover the expanded field. There is still a gap between the professional artist and the recreational weaver, but they are talking. People are still debating craft versus art, and the word *craft* is being dropped from the terminology and names of some museums and schools. Despite all this, information is more widely available and shared, and fiber arts are more visible than ever.

Rob Pulleyn, who started *Fiberarts* magazine in 1974, wanted to blend respect for the traditional with an enthusiasm for the new, because he saw a disconnect between art and craft in a fiber field that was filled with energy but lacked focus. He published a tabloid-size magazine for customers of a yarn shop in Albuquerque, New Mexico, and it became one of the premier magazines in the field. In his retirement editorial (spring 2004), Pulleyn saw a "resurgence of interest in fibers . . . more readers, more advertisers, more galleries and more energy than I can remember."[2] He predicted that the next decade would see the forgotten craft medium move from the wings to center stage.

Jurors at the recent fiber shows held in Michigan have expressed their surprise and pleasure at the wide range of techniques, the high quality, and the creativity of the Michigan weavers and fiber artists whose work is entered in these shows. Teachers who come to the state's workshops after many years on the national circuit frequently say they love to come to Michigan because of the high quality of work by students in their classes. While

Michigan's development of modern handweaving has reflected the national trends in the field, it has also often been a leader, with schools and craft- and art-centered community activities that encourage good work. Michigan has been one of the most active states in promoting handweaving, inviting distinguished fiber artists to lecture, teach, and critique local work. The longevity and vibrancy of Michigan's handweaving tradition is due in no small way to the many individuals who built that tradition, volunteered to make the guilds work, and taught at all levels, from private to university, as well as to the local yarn shops, art centers, art organizations, galleries, and museums that support fiber events and provide opportunities for growth. Hosting the national convergence of the Handweavers Guild of America in 2006 in Grand Rapids continues Michigan's tradition of outreach and influence in the fiber world.

Afterword

The MLH History Project

Often, an idea needs a long time to incubate—to germinate and grow. This was the case with the inspiration for *Fascination with Fiber.* As a young girl growing up on a farm in New Jersey, I learned most of the major fiber crafts from my mother, beginning with the embroidering of a sampler. I sat at my mother's knee, so to speak, and gradually learned all the other skills of needlework, knitting, and crocheting. I often did the hand finishing of clothing my mother had sewn for me and my siblings. I loved the companionable and rewarding process of working with her then—and now—in making a new garment from cloth.

It was not until I moved to Grand Rapids, Michigan, that I learned to weave. From the very first night of class in the local weaving shop, I knew that weaving held a fascination for me. To take some strands of yarn and, through some magical process, create fabric was part of the fascination. The movement was rhythmic and soothing; the yarns were soft to the touch. Even dressing the loom became a meditative process. I was encouraged to join the local guild—another place to meet weavers and learn new skills. In Lansing, where I had a new home and a new job, the guild was like a second family—a different community of new friends with similar interests. Here I could learn. Here I was supported and encouraged to try new things, to work and excel in my new craft.

Apart from weaving, I love things from the past—textiles, clothing, household items and objects—and want to learn about people who lived before me and how they lived their lives. As I continued weaving, I began to wonder more about the guilds and weavers in Michigan who preceded me. Who were they? Why did they form guilds? Why did they weave?

The culmination of the idea for the handweaving history project happened very suddenly. I had mentioned my interest to Kurt Dewhurst, the director of the Michigan State University Museum, and not long after, a special grant in state arts and culture became available. Knowing of my interest, Dewhurst and other museum staff encouraged me to pursue my idea. As a member of the Michigan League of Handweavers, I felt this would be a worthwhile project for the organization. The MLH board heartily agreed. Funding for a pilot project to research and document the hand-weaving history of MLH and its guilds was sought by applying for the grant. A flurry of planning and work followed, involving writing the grant and arranging a workshop for the training of members from five guilds located geographically throughout Michigan. The grant was awarded to the MLH, and plans for the Michigan League of Handweavers History Project proceeded. Recording equipment, tapes, cameras and film, and guild kits were purchased. Invitations were sent to guilds, and phone calls were made, inviting members to participate in the in-depth study of their guild's history through this project.

In April 1998, the first meeting of officers from the MLH, MSU Museum staff, and representatives of five Michigan guilds (the Greater Lansing Weavers Guild, the Weavers Guild of Kalamazoo, the Buellwood Weavers Guild, the Midland FiberArts Guild, and the Michigan Weavers Guild) took place at the MSU Museum. Museum historians and specialists in folk art provided training in historical research methods and folklife research, including oral history. All the tools and materials needed for the research were provided; goals, deadlines, and the format of the research project were discussed, determined, and set. The group met three months later to share their research results and planned a small exhibit featuring the project, which opened at the Lansing Art Gallery in October 1998 in conjunction with the MLH Biennial Fiber Show. A minigrant was awarded for the preparation and mounting of this exhibit, another successful collaboration between the MLH and the MSU Museum. The small exhibit then traveled to guild meetings throughout the state, including UP Exchange Day, with the hope that guilds would want to learn more about their histories and participate.

The pilot project had many goals, including the establishment at the MSU Museum of a central state archives for the oral histories and historical documentation resulting from this project and future research, as a resource for future researchers. Another goal was to mount a large exhibition after the completion of the research of Michigan's handweaving history. During the following three years, additional meetings for training were held, and all the state's guilds were contacted to help in the process of documenting their guild's history. When most of the documentation was completed, the decision was made to develop a major exhibition at the MSU Museum.

The process of developing and installing a large exhibition involves a substantial commitment of time, money, collaboration, and dedication. Members of the MLH and the MSU Museum wished to make the public aware of Michigan's rich handweaving history and its vibrant presence in today's fiber arts. A meeting of key MSU staff and the MLH research team of about twelve members was held at the MSU Museum in September 2001 to discuss the various components of the exhibition, programming, fund-raising, and the tasks to be accomplished. The unique comprehensive exhibition would include a number of smaller exhibits: a historic exhibit tracing handweaving in Michigan from statehood in 1837 to the present, including a historic photo album of all the guilds in the MLH; a contemporary juried fiber show and an invitational show for faculty in the fiber arts; a studio space for the demonstration of weaving and spinning, which included plant and animal fibers to touch and accompanying information; a community loom on which the public could try weaving and create a community tapestry; and a large, eight-foot-square fiber map of Michigan, made by the guilds in the MLH.

An opening date in early 2004 for the exhibit at the MSU Museum was discussed and decided, and a time frame was established for the completion of the work ahead. As the Handweavers Guild of America was to hold its 2006 convergence in Grand Rapids, with the MLH hosting the conference, everyone felt it would be important that the exhibition, which would run through December 2004 and travel to other venues after being hosted at the MSU Museum, should conclude at the convergence.

With our work schedule in hand, the first major task of fund-raising began in the spring of 2002. Substantial funds were needed before applying for grants to develop and install this major traveling exhibition and to build the traveling cases that would be needed. MLH members and guilds and other fiber-related organizations and friends were very supportive of the fund-raising efforts, and the needed funds were raised.

Throughout the two-and-a-half years of work and research, progress reports were made at MLH board meetings and in newsletters. Stories and information were gathered from members of guilds working on their guild's history. Museums were contacted as potential hosts for the upcoming traveling exhibition. Textiles, objects, and images were searched for and located to represent historic time periods, guild projects, and important weavers. Exhibition text panels and object labels were written. Graphics were designed. Professor Sigrid Wortmann Weltge, renowned for her research and writing about the Bauhaus weavers and artists, was invited to judge the MLH Thirteenth Biennial Fiber Show and to present a lecture at the opening reception. Brochures and entry forms were designed to announce the juried fiber show, including information about the length of the exhibit and lending period. Entries were judged in February 2004, and a month later, the exhibition opened to the public. In April, Weltge returned to East Lansing for the opening reception and awards ceremony and presented her lecture "Bauhaus Women: Pioneers of Modern Textile Design" to a full house.

A variety of public programs related to the project were planned and held primarily at the MSU Museum. The opening reception featured the Weltge lecture and gallery tours by curator Marie Gile. A sheep-to-shawl event was held in May, with sheep provided by the MSU farms. A daylong conservation workshop entitled "Textiles of Yesterday and Today" was held later in May, with additional afternoon programs at the MSU Museum and at MSU's College of Human Ecology. A PowerPoint lecture about hand-weaving in Hartland—entitled "Things Useful and Beautiful"—was presented in June. In a special collaborative event in September, members of the MLH, staff from the MSU Museum and from MSU's Department of Campus Park and Planning and Department of Animal Sciences, and individuals involved in raising fiber-bearing animals (who brought their alpacas and llamas) came together for an afternoon of education, dyeing, spinning, and weaving in the W. J. Beal Botanical Garden at MSU. The programming concluded in late November 2004 with "Rags, Rugs, and Weavers," a presentation on the time-honored craft of rag rug weaving.

The exhibition would not have been possible without the dynamic energy of many members of the MLH research team and the MSU Museum staff—who helped with research, the developing and mounting of the exhibition, and programming—or without the many MLH and guild members who volunteered their time and talents in this effort, demonstrating weaving and spinning for the public and participating in many other activities. Wonderful new friendships were forged across the state and beyond as part of this fulfilling project. Because of the very positive public response to the exhibition, a decision was made to go one step further—to write this book, a labor of love.

Marie A. Gile

Textiles and Objects in the Historic FASCINATION WITH FIBER Exhibit

Framed fabric swatches	ca. 1816–17	Linen and cotton, maker unknown
Hatchel	1822	Wood and metal, maker unknown
Spinning wheel	ca. 1830–40	Oak and maple, maker unknown
Table cover	1840	Linen, "Woven by Great Grandfather Ross"
Hand towel	ca. 1840	Linen, maker unknown
Hand towel	ca. 1840	Linen and cotton, maker unknown
Coverlet	1844	Wool, Abram Van Doren
Sley hook	pre-1872	Wood, maker unknown
Niddy noddy	pre-1918	Wood, maker unknown
Pair of wool carders	pre-1918	Wood and metal, maker unknown
Shuttle Service bulletin	1935	Edited by Osma Gallinger of Cromaine Crafts
Rag rug	1938	Cotton, Mrs. Henry Kehus
Bedspread, overshot pattern	ca. 1930s	Wool, "Hand-made by Cromaine"
Boat and stick shuttles	ca. 1930s	Wood, Cromaine Crafts
Bobbins for shuttle	ca. 1930s	Metal, Cromaine Crafts
Brochure	ca. 1930s	Paper, Cromaine Crafts
Afghan, overshot pattern	ca. late 1930s	Wool, maker unknown
Floor loom, four-shaft	ca. 1939	Wood, Cromaine Crafts
Hand towel	ca. 1930s–1940s	Cotton, Cromaine Crafts/Hartland Area Crafts
Napkins	ca. 1930s–1940s	Cotton, Hartland Area Crafts
Skirt	ca. 1930s–1940s	Cotton, Ann Hooker
Table runners	ca. 1930s–1940s	Cotton, Cromaine Crafts/Hartland Area Crafts
Towels	ca. 1930s–1940s	Cotton, Cromaine Crafts/Hartland Area Crafts

Chimayo weaving	ca. 1940	Wool, Chimayo weavers of Chimayo, NM, and John B. Davidson Woolen Mill
Table mat	ca. 1940	Linen and wool, Studio Loja Saarinen
Wool sample card	1941	John B. Davidson Woolen Mill
Hearthside manual	1942	Nellie Johnson
Pin for excellence	1942	Metal
Identification badge no. 69	ca. 1942	Metal, Clinton Wool Mill
Inside Story booklet	1944	Clinton Wool Mill
Rag rug	1944	Cotton and wool, Mrs. Makkimaa
Drapery fabric	ca. 1948	Cotton and synthetics, Fred Wessels
Booklet of sample yarns	ca. 1950s	Hughes Fawcett, Inc.
Handweaving sample	ca. 1950s	Cotton, Dorothea Buell
Hobby-Knit Machine	ca. 1950s	Montello Products Company, motorized by Fred Wessels
Practical Weaving Suggestions pamphlet	ca. 1950s	Lily Mills Company
Purse	ca. 1950s	Acrylic handles, cottons, and synthetics, Loretta Nichols
Seprasox and box	ca. 1950s	Wool and leather, John B. Davidson Woolen Mill
Shirt	ca. 1950s	Wool, Melvina McGarr
Towels and napkins	ca. 1950s	Cotton, Ruth Scherer
Upholstery fabric	ca. 1950s	Linen, cotton, wool, and nylon, Robert Sailors
Yarn swatches and price list	ca. 1950s	Lily Mills Company
Price list	1952	John P. Bexell and Son
Woven handbag	ca. late 1950s	Cotton, linen, and wool, Loretta Nichols
Luncheon tablecloth	ca. 1950–60	Cotton, Mary Sayler
Four purses	ca. 1950–61	Wool, cotton, and metallics, Michigan Weavers Guild
Rag rug	ca. 1955	Cotton and cotton tubing, Fred Wessels
Drapery fabric	ca. 1955–60	Silk, Marianne Strengell
Two fabric samples	ca. 1956	Synthetics and metallics, Marianne Strengell
Shuttle-Craft portfolio	1957	Harriet Tidball
Two wooden reed hooks	ca. 1959	Fred Wessels
Brochure and handbook	1960	Michigan League of Handweavers
Five matchboxes	1960	Handwoven fabric on matchbox(es), Greater Lansing Weavers Guild
Four barrettes	1960	Handwoven fabric on wood, Ann Arbor Fiberarts Guild

Name tag	1960	Handwoven fabric, Michigan League of Handweavers
Baseball (cutout view)	ca. 1960	Unspun and spun wool and leather, John B. Davidson Woolen Mill
Brochure	ca. 1960	Waldenwoods
Coat	ca. 1960	Wool and mohair, Gladys Brophil Wonnacott
Fabric sample	ca. 1960	Cotton and synthetics, Fred Wessels
Pillows, two	ca. 1960	Wool, Libby Crawford
Place mat and napkin	ca. 1960	Linen, Muriel Neeland
Untitled, wall hanging	ca. 1960	Wool, Libby Crawford
Wall hanging, fern	ca. 1960	Wool, Jean Wilson
The Weaver's Book	1961	Harriet Tidball
Fabric for a dress	1962	Wool, Mary Sayler
Shuttle-Craft portfolios	1962, 1963, 1966, 1968	Harriet Tidball
Fabric sample	ca. 1966	Natural fibers and grasses, Marianne Strengell
Rug sample	ca. 1966	Linen, cotton, wool, and nylon, Robert Sailors
Mailbag	1967	Cotton and linen, Frederick J. Fawcett
Wall hanging, fern	ca. late 1960s	Linen, Theo Moorman
Minidress	1970	Cotton, Kati Meek
Color-and-Weave	ca. 1970	Margaret and Thomas Windeknecht
Greeting card	ca. 1970	Cotton and metallics, Ruth Cross
Wall hanging, fern	ca. 1970	Cotton, Nancy Searles
Wall hanging, fern	ca. 1970	Cotton and wool, Ruth Scherer
Weaving sample	ca. 1970	Cotton, Ann Arbor Fiberarts Guild
Weaving sample	ca. 1970	Metal, Carol Noffz
Convergence program	1972	Handweavers Guild of America
Alternatives to a Fig Leaf	ca. 1972	Barbara Wittenberg
Shawl	ca. 1972	Cotton, Martha Brownscombe
Man's bog shirt	1975	Wool, Karen Krause
Bookmark	ca. 1975	Cotton, Muriel Neeland
Laughter wall hanging	1976	Wool and linen, Margaret Windeknecht
Untitled wall hanging	1976	Rovana (synthetic), mylar, metal, plastic tubes, and linen, Robert Kidd
Blanket	1978	Wool, Alice and Howard Griswold
Child's poncho vest	1978	Wool, Karen Krause
Fabric	1978	Cotton, wool, rayon, mohair, metallics, mylar, and viscose, Robert Sailors

Arctic Night wall hanging	ca. 1980	Linen, wool, and metallics, Elizabeth Leifer
Seed Pod wall hanging	ca. 1980	Linen, wool, and pearls, Katherine Ux
Child's coat	1981	Wool, Pat Chipman
Purse	1985	Silk, Ruth Whitmyer
Slits and Extensions wall hanging	1985	Wool, Millie Danielson
Baby blanket	ca. 1985	Wool, Alice and Howard Griswold
Kimono	ca. 1985	Wool and cotton, designed by JoAnn Bachelder, handwoven squares by Midland FiberArts Guild study group
Place mat	ca. 1985	Cotton, Ethel Alexander
Guardians of the New Day wall panel	1987	Cotton, linen, and mylar, Gerhardt Knodel
Rag rug	1988	Cotton and wool, Johanna Pohjala
Three bookmarks	1990s	Cotton, Carol Isleib
Wedding dress bodice	1991	Silk and beads, Karen East
Lady tapestry	1992	Wool, Karen Yackell
Towel	1994	Cotton, Anne Westlund
Anasazi tapestry	1995	Wool and linen, Millie Danielson
Summer Nights pillow case	1995	Linen, Kati Meek
Garden of the Full Moon wall hanging	1996	Hand-dyed wool, JoAnn Bachelder
Christening gown and hat	1997	Silk and cotton, Esther James
The Presence of Absence Is Everywhere wall hanging	2001	Wools, cottons, silk, rayon, and metallics, Kathy Zasuwa
Table runner	2001	Cotton, Lestra Hazel
Sweater jacket	2002	Wool, mohair, and synthetics (woven body and knitted sleeves and trim), Brenda Mergen
Towel	2002	Cotton, Sue Peters
Red Tree Alert	2003	Natural and synthetic fibers, Roz Berlin
Table runner	2004	Cotton, Leslie Johnson

List of Contemporary Art in the FASCINATION WITH FIBER Exhibit

Each artwork listed is a wall hanging unless otherwise noted.

Color Works 3	Kathleen Alfonso	Rayon and cotton
Autumn Mosaic	Ken Allen	Hand-painted rayon, scarf
Bronze Tessalation	Ken Allen	Pearl cotton and silk, scarf
Winter Rose	Ken Allen	Rayon, scarf
Bog Jacket	Pamela Arquette	Wool with commercial lining, jacket
Double Diamonds	Pamela Arquette	Wool and alpaca, scarf
Painted Diamonds	Pamela Arquette	Silk, scarf
Transformation	Jill Ault	Silk, rayon, linen, and polyester
Aerial View	JoAnn Bachelder	Wool
Between the Rocks	JoAnn Bachelder	Wool
Landscape in Yellow	JoAnn Bachelder	Wool
Shomon: The World of Learning	Betty Bahen	Cotton
Seasonal Blocks	Mary Lou Gleason Best	Cotton, scarf
Michigan Pines	Gisela Bosch	Cotton and rayon
It Happens So Gradual	Martha Brownscombe	Rayon chenille
Scarf	Ronda Cardwell	Rayon, scarf
Progression	Susan Cayton	Silk
Sampler	Susan Cayton	Dyed silk
Lifelines	Betty Christians	Wool, rug
Descent	Joanne Cromley	Hand-dyed wool and cotton
Illumination	Joanne Cromley	Hand-dyed silk, silk bouclé, and wool
Scandinavia Revisited	Millie Danielson	Wool and cotton, tapestry
St. Katherine's Light	Karen East	Silk
Log Cabin Wrap	Mary Fechner	Merino, silk, and tencel, stole

Winter Stars	Mary Fechner	Merino, silk, and rayon, scarf
Hall Runner	Hedi Frazier	Berber wool, rug
Cherry Orchards and Bay— Traverse City, Michigan	Marie Gile	Hand-dyed cotton and synthetics
Vernal Cross	Marie Gile	Hand-dyed cotton and synthetics
Fascination A	Linda Griffith	Cotton and wool, afghan
Fascination B	Linda Griffith	Cotton and wool, afghan
Scarf	Helen Griffiths	Cotton, silk, rayon, and wool, scarf
Scarf	Helen Griffiths	Rayon chenille, scarf
Wall Hanging	Helen Griffiths	Wire
Dark Currents	Lestra Hazel	Rayon and cotton, table runner
Homage To Klee	Lestra Hazel	Cotton
Midnight Rain	Lestra Hazel	Silk, scarf
Fractured Paisley	Gretchen Huggett	Cotton and polyester, scarf
Ikat and Knots	Gretchen Huggett	Tencel, cotton, stole
Melon	Gretchen Huggett	Cotton and polyester, scarf
Perpendicular Pulsations	Bonnie Kay	Tencel
A Wedding Handkerchief	Mary Lou Koval	Cotton and linen, bobbin lace handkerchief
Splendid Table	Elizabeth Leifer	Linen, rayon, and spun paper, table runner and six place mats
Circus	Priscilla Lynch	Cotton and wool, tapestry
It Takes a Village	Priscilla Lynch	Cotton and wool, tapestry
Striped Red Rug	Lynda MacHaila	Wool, rug
Red Alert	Marion Marzolf	Silk, cotton, and horsehair
Wishing On the Stars	Marion Marzolf	Wool, linen, and silk
My Cat Allergy	Lynn Mayne	Wool and cotton, tapestry
A Rainbow Mat	Cathy McCarthy	Cotton and acrylic, mat
Silk Fascination	Cathy McCarthy	Silk, scarf
Silk Fascination II	Cathy McCarthy	Silk, scarf
Scarf	Lois McCorvie	Hand-dyed silk, scarf
Moon Indigo	Marcia McDonald	Cotton
Baltic Cheer	Kati Meek	Linen singles, toweling
Cush Your Tush x 2	Kati Meek	Wool and mixed fiber, pillows
Thank-You Charles Rennie MacIntosh	Kati Meek	Wool
Blue Bucket Bag and Mittens	Loretta Oliver	Felted wool and stitchery, purse and mittens
Cross Dyed III	Loretta Oliver	Cotton, lyocel, silk, and wool, scarf
Red Hot Bag	Loretta Oliver	Felted wool and stitchery, purse

Karst Mountain Scarf	Nancy Peck	Cotton, scarf
Twisted Ribbon Fabric	Nancy Peck	Cotton and silk, scarf
Red, Yellow, Blue: One Warp, Three Wefts	Sue Peters	Tencel, cotton, and polyester, three scarves
Shapes: Color and Weave Twill	Sue Peters	Linen, table runner
All That Glitters	Roxanne Pett	Cotton and beading, necklace
Scarf That Went Bump	Roxanne Pett	Wool, scarf
Through the Woods	Monica Prince	Cotton and silk
When I Was Size 5	Judith Puotinen	Wool, wool felt, beads, and silk, kimono
Southwest	Mary Rappuhn	Gourd and beads, container
Numo Felted Scarf	Laura Seligman	Felted wool felt, scarf
Ritual Vestment	Laura Seligman	Felted wool and beads, clerical stole
Whispers	Carol Stygles	Wool, vintage chiffon, and quilted cotton
Midas Touch	Patricia Thompson	Paper, paint, and cotton, purse
Midas Touch IV	Patricia Thompson	Paper and cotton
Spirits of the Indigo Sea	Patricia Thompson	Paper and cotton
Make New Friends but Keep the Old, One Is Silver, the Other Gold	Mary Underwood	Cotton, linen, and metallics, runner
Nocturna	Margaret Windeknecht	Silk, cotton, and glass beads
Reprise	Margaret Windeknecht	Silk, cotton, and glass beads
Sonata	Margaret Windeknecht	Silk, cotton, and glass beads
River of Change—China	Karen Yackell	Wool, rayon, silk, and cotton, tapestry
The Elements: Fire, Earth, Air, Water	Mimi Zoet-Cummings	Hand-dyed wool and linen, rug
Flight	Mimi Zoet-Cummings	Handspun wool and linen, rug
Lines and Squares	Mimi Zoet-Cummings	Wool and linen, rug

Guilds in the
Michigan League of Handweavers

Guild	City	E-mail Address
Ann Arbor Fiberarts Guild	Ann Arbor	milleed@umich.edu
AuSable Manistee Fiber Guild	Grayling	hassanl@kirtland.cc.mi.us
Black Sheep Weavers' Fiber Guild	Howell	jmillies@joimail.com
Black Swamp Spinner's Guild	Clyde, OH	caytonsj@juno.com
Buellwood Weavers Guild	Rockland	speerj@up.net
Country Spinners and Bridge Shuttlers	Brimley	sspiewak@up.net
Cross Border Weavers	Bloomfield Hills	suewalton@comcast.net
Delta Spinners	Escanaba	vkill@up.net
Detroit Handweavers and Spinners	Clawson	grschalm@aol.com
Eastside Handweavers Guild	Grosse Pointe Woods	cgreenfelder@comcast.net
FinnWeavers Fiber Guild	Royal Oak	dova@msn.com
Fort Wayne Weavers Guild	Fort Wayne, IN	jbopp4@comcast.net
Friends of the Fleece	Applegate	lentzcb@aol.com
Genesee Valley Fiber Guild	Flint	joettaweaver@aol.com
Greater Lansing Weavers Guild	Eaton Rapids	johns149@msu.edu
Jackson Handweavers Guild	Springport	oldmillyarn@acd.net
Lake Charlevoix Area Guild	Boyne City	holly@shaltzfarm.com
Lakeshore Fiber Arts Guild	Byron Center	jennifergoulddesigns@hotmail.com
Michigan Handspinners Guild	Livonia	rallen7468@aol.com
Michigan Weavers Guild	Farmington Hills	jacketaylor@twmi.rr.com
Midland FiberArts Guild	Midland	rhphill@sbcglobal.net
Mill Race Weavers Guild	Waterford	kkemmer@campbell-ewald.com
Niles Handweavers Guild	South Haven	larmidgelewis@verizon.net

Guild	City	E-mail Address
Nor'craft Weavers Guild	Ludington	apettig@charter.net
Northeast Michigan Weavers Guild	Alpena	krmeek@charter.net
Northland Weavers	Traverse City	mcc@traverse.com
North Oakland Handweavers Guild	Rochester Hills	
Spiderwoman Handspinners	Marquette	vkill@up.net
Sunrise Spinning Guild	Rose City	kritterkeeper@m33access.com
Toledo Area Weavers Guild	Sylvania, OH	glover@buckeye-express.com
Town and Country Weavers	Dearborn	klaycock@peoplepc.com
Weavers Guild of Kalamazoo	Kalamazoo	cmccarth@kresanet.org
Woodland Weavers and Spinners	Grand Rapids	lynneswets@sbcglobal.net
Yarnwinders Fiber Guild	Marquette	yarnwinder98@yahoo.com

Presidents of the Michigan League of Handweavers

1959	Helen Hill
1961	Joyce Jones
1963	Ayliffe Ochs
1965	Renah Green
1967	Annora Gardner
1971	Alice Matthews
1973	Mary Sayler
1975	Verda Elliott
1977	Louise Piranian
1979	Brenda Mergen
1981	Mary Sayler
1982	Patti Aiken
1983	JoAnn Bachelder
1985	Kathy Zasuwa
1987	Charlene Hancock
1989	Martha Town
1991	Peggy Adams
1993	Priscilla Lynch
1995	Nancy Peck
1997	Lestra Hazel
1999	Sue Peters
2001	Marion Marzolf
2003	Martha Brownscombe
2005	Karen Krause

Notes

Chapter 1

1. Kax Wilson, *A History of Textiles* (Boulder, CO: Westview Press, 1979), 236–37.

2. Wilson, *History*, 199.

3. *Michigan: A Guide to the Wolverine State* (New York: Oxford University Press, 1941), 55, 136.

4. Informal conversations with author Marion Marzolf during the University of Michigan Cancer Center Art Therapy project, winter 2004.

5. Mary Meigs Atwater, *The Shuttle-Craft Book of American Handweaving* (New York: Macmillan, 1947), 67.

6. Mrs. Sarah E. Soper, "Reminiscence of Pioneer Life in Oakland County," *Michigan Historical Collections* 28 (1897–98), 408.

7. Ruth Hoppin, "Personal Recollections of Pioneer Days," *Michigan Historical Collections* 38 (1909–11), 416.

8. Eric Broudy, *The Book of Looms* (Hanover, NH: University Press of New England, 1979), 153.

9. Frank B. Woodford and Albert Hyma, *Gabriel Richard, Frontier Ambassador* (Detroit: Wayne State University Press, 1958), 88.

10. Dave Pennington, *A Pictorial Guide to American Spinning Wheels* (Sabbath Lake, ME: Shaker Press, 1975), 30, 61.

11. David W. Penney, *Native Arts of North America* (Paris: Editions Pierre Terrail, 1998), 57–70; Carrie A. Lyford, *Ojibwa Crafts* (1943; reprint, Stevens Point, WI: R. Schneider, 1982); Jennifer Harris, ed., *5000 Years of Textiles* (New York: Harry N. Abrams, 1993), 267–69.

12. Clarita S. Anderson, *Weaving a Legacy: The Don and Jean Stuck Coverlet Collection* (Columbus, OH: Columbus Museum of Art and Harry N. Abrams, 1995), 15.

13. Katharine McGregor Brown, "Michigan's Pioneer Coverlet Weaver: A Study of Abram William Van Doren's Seven Years of Coverlet Weaving in Avon Township, Michigan, 1844 to 1851" (Master's thesis, Wayne State University, 1982), 17–19, 60.

14. Brown, "Michigan's Pioneer Coverlet Weaver," 59.

15. Brown, "Michigan's Pioneer Coverlet Weaver," 8, 13.

16. Katharine Brown, "Fancy Coverlet Weaving," *Michigan History*, May/June 1987, 14–15.

17. Brown, "Michigan's Pioneer Coverlet Weaver," 74.

18. U.S. Tariff Commission, *The Wool Growing Industry* (Washington: U.S. Government Printing Office, 1921), 13–14, 113.

19. Norman L. Crockett, *The Woolen Industry of the Midwest* (Lexington: University Press of Kentucky, 1970), 108.

20. *Wool Production* (Lansing, MI: Michigan Crop Reporting Service, 1976).

21. Sandra Sageser Clark, "Clip, Card, Spin, and Weave," *Michigan History*, July/August 1984, 38–39.

22. "Cloth Making Fast Growing Industry at Highland Park," *Ford News*, March 22, 1926, 3.

23. "Upholstery on the Hoof," *Ford News*, September 8, 1927, 4–5.

24. "The Textile Industry of Michigan," undated magazine clipping, Historical Society of Clinton, Clinton Township Public Library, Village of Clinton.

25. Clara Squires and Jean Kline, *Island City Pictorial History, 1835–1980* (Eaton Rapids, MI, Squires, 1980).

26. Linton Davidson, interview by Marion Marzolf, May 15, 2002, transcript, Michigan League of Handweavers History Project Collection, Michigan State University Museum, East Lansing, MI (hereafter cited as MLH History Project Collection, MSU Museum).

27. Dedication program for Clinton Woolen Mill marker, May 17, 1980, Clinton Township Public Library, Clinton, MI.

28. Kathy and Gary Zeilinger, interview by Marion Marzolf, June 17, 2002, transcript, MLH History Project Collection, MSU Museum.

29. *The Belding Brothers*, pamphlet, Belding Brothers Collection, Belding Historical Museum, Belding, MI.

30. Barbara Havira, "At Work in Belding," *Michigan History*, May/June 1965, 33–41.

Chapter 2

1. Alda Ganze Kaye, "Weaver Rose, A New Perspective," *Shuttle Spindle and Dyepot* (hereafter SS&D), spring 1977, 16.

2. Ford R. Bryan, *Beyond the Model T* (Detroit: Wayne State University Press, 1980), chap. 18 "The Educator"; visitor tour guide notebooks, Henry Ford Archives, Benson Ford Research Center.

3. Alice K. Waagen, "An Historical Survey and Analysis of American Handweaving" (PhD diss., Pennsylvania State University, 1982), chap. 3.

4. Philis Alvic, *Weavers of the Southern Highlands* (Lexington: University Press of Kentucky, 2003).

5. Clara Belle Thompson and Margaret Lukes Wise, "How to Make Money at Home: The 1941 Way," *Woman's Day*, May 1941, 11–13, 52–53, 71, 73–75.

6. Thompson and Wise, "Money at Home," 11.

7. Janet Meany and Paula Pfaff, *Rag Rug Handbook* (Loveland, CO: Interweave Press, 1996), 96–97; undated clippings, Willard Library, Battle Creek, MI.

8. Mary Jo Reiter, *Weaving a Life: The Story of Mary Meigs Atwater* (Loveland, CO: Interweave Press, 1992); *Handweaver and Craftsman*, fall 1964.

9. *Shuttle-Craft Guild Bulletin*, September 1924, 1.

10. Betty A. Biehl, "Mary Atwater: A Daughter Remembers," *Handwoven*, May/June 1990, 39.

11. *Shuttle-Craft Guild Bulletin*, September 1924, 1.

12. *Shuttle-Craft Guild Bulletin*, September 1929, 1.

13. *Shuttle-Craft Guild Bulletin*, August 1938, 1.

14. Ruth E. Cross, "A Little about the Personal Mary Atwater and the Conference of American Handweavers," *Fiber Connection* (Michigan League of Handweavers) 20,

no. 1 (fall 1980): 4–5. In the 1930s, flying by airplane was still a novel occurrence, as evidenced by Ruth Cross's comments and by comments about Mary Atwater's mode of travel in the *Livingston County Press* (undated clipping, ca. 1938, Hartland Area Historical Society, Hartland, MI).

15. *Handweaver and Craftsman*, fall 1964; MLH Newsletter, fall 1960, 2.

16. Harriet Tidball, "Industry Looks to Handweaver for Inspiration, Says Expert," *Portland Oregon Reporter*, March 31, 1962.

17. Harriet Tidball, *Contemporary Tapestry*, Shuttle Craft Monograph Twelve (Lansing, MI: Shuttle Craft Guild, 1964), 45. Eva Anttila came to the United States in the summer of 1963 at Tidball's invitation. Two ten-day workshops were held: the first at Waldenwoods in Hartland, Michigan, and the second at Boulder, Montana.

18. Peter Collingwood later published *The Techniques of Rug Weaving* (1969), the rug weaver's bible, which has been reprinted eleven times and is now in paperback; *The Techniques of Sprang* (1974); *The Techniques of Tablet Weaving* (1982); *The Maker's Hand* (1987); *Rug Weaving Techniques: Beyond the Basics* (1990); and *The Techniques of Ply-Split Braiding* (2004).

19. "Eva Anttila of Finland Stresses Design in Her Tapestry Workshops," *Handweaver and Craftsman*, winter 1964, 16–17, 47.

20. Greater Lansing Weavers Guild, Loom crafters, and Niles Handweavers Guild Papers, MLH History Project Collection, MSU Museum; "Swedish Weaver to Lecture at East Lansing March 28," *Lansing State Journal*, March 7, 1961, 16.

21. William S. Colburn, e-mail communication to Marie Gile, April 26, 2005.

22. Mary Sayler, "Harriet Tidball and the Michigan League of Handweavers," *Fiber Connection* 20, no. 1 (fall 1980): 6; "In Memory: Mary Sayler," *Fiber Connection* 41, no. 3 (spring 2001): 5; Mary Sayler, interview by Lestra Hazel, June 11, 1998.

23. Virginia I. Harvey, "Harriet Tidball," *SS&D*, fall 1977, 4–6; "Hand Weaving Authority Visits," *Montana Standard-Post*, March 29, 1962, 12.

24. Harriet Tidball, *Contemporary Costume: Strictly Handwoven*, Shuttle Craft Monograph Twenty Four (Lansing, MI: Shuttle Craft Guild, 1968).

25. Sayler, interview.

26. "Women's Features," *Lansing State Journal*, March 28, 1961, 12.

27. Elizabeth Clark, interview by Lestra Hazel, February 17, 1999, transcript, MLH History Project Collection, MSU Museum.

28. Harriet Tidball, *Supplementary Warp Patterning*, Shuttle Craft Monograph Seventeen (Lansing, MI: Shuttle Craft Guild, 1966), 31. The remaining sources cited in this note are from the MLH History Project Collection at the MSU Museum: *Ontario Handweavers and Spinners Bulletin* 12, no. 2 (December 1968); ExCo '68 conference brochure, 1968; "The Gampers: Textile Explorers," four-page speech by the Gampers for presentation at ExCo '68, undated; "Recollections from Verda Elliott [member of the Gampers starting in 1972]", undated.

Chapter 3

1. Hartland Area Historical Society, *Hartland: Weaving the Past with the Present* (Hartland, MI: Hartland Area Historical Society, 2004), 71–72.

2. Patti Aikin, "Waldenwoods: Weaving in Hartland," ms, undated, Collections of Cromaine District Library, Hartland, MI.

3. Hartland Area Historical Society, *Hartland*, 115.

4. Aikin, "Waldenwoods."

5. Quoted in D. James Galbraith, *Hartland: Change in the Heart of America* (Hartland, MI: Galbraith-Scott Publications, ca. 1985), 55.

6. Jo Graham, "Recollections of a Weaver: Jo Graham," *Fiber Connection* 22, no. 2 (winter 1983): 3.

7. Muriel Neeland, interview by Marie Gile, June 25, 1998, transcript, MLH History Project Collection, MSU Museum.

8. Neeland, interview.

9. "News from Summer Weaving Institute," *Homeweaver* (Cromaine Crafts), March/April 1938.

10. Ruth E. Cross, "A Little about the Personal Mary Atwater and the Conference of American Handweavers," *Fiber Connection* 20, no. 1 (fall 1980): 4–5.

11. Wendy Landry, lecture on Mary Black, HGA convergence, Vancouver, Canada, 2004. Landry is working on a study of Black's life and work—especially in Nova Scotia, where Black was born and settled. The lecture was published in *Occupational Therapy and Rehabilitation* 17, no. 6 (December 1938).

12. Reiter, *Weaving a Life*, 63, 143–48, 155.

13. Clifford G. Lindahl, interview by Marion Marzolf, March 20, 2003, Hartland, MI, transcript, MLH History Project Collection, MSU Museum.

14. Lindahl, interview.

15. "Weavers and Weaving Shops: Mrs. E. C. Ochs at Hartland Area Crafts," *Warp and Weft* 9, no. 9 (November 1958), 3, 6.

16. "Minutes of Organization Committee for the Michigan League of Handweavers—Conference Meeting," July 24, 1959, MLH History Project Collection, MSU Museum.

Chapter 4

1. Joy Hakonson Colby, "The Detroit Society of Arts and Crafts, 1906–1976: An Introduction," in Susan F. Rossen, ed., *Arts and Crafts in Detroit, 1906–1976: The Movement, the Society, the School* (Detroit: Detroit Institute of Arts, 1976), 64.

2. Colby, "Detroit Society of Arts and Crafts," 66.

3. Robert Judson Clark, "Cranbrook and the Search for Twentieth-Century Form," in Robert Judson Clark et al., *Design in America: The Cranbrook Vision, 1925–50* (New York: Harry N. Abrams, 1983), 26–30.

4. Christa C. Mayer Thurman, "Textiles," in Clark et al., *Design in America*, 175; papers of Loja Saarinen, Lillian Holm, and Ruth Ingvarson, Cranbrook Archives, Cranbrook Academy of Art, Bloomfield Hills, MI.

5. Jane Patrick, "The Cranbrook Loom," *Handwoven*, September/October 2002, 67.

6. Mark Coir, "Lillian Holm: Creator of an Artistic Legacy," *Tradition*, n.d., 24–25, Cranbrook Archives, Cranbrook Academy of Art, Bloomfield Hills, MI.

7. Lois Bryant, interview by Marion Marzolf, October 16, 2004.

8. Jack Lenor Larsen, "At the Cranbrook Academy of Art," *Handweaver and Craftsman*, spring 1952, 24.

9. Strengell Papers, Cranbrook Archives, Cranbrook Academy of Art, Bloomfield Hills, MI.

10. Dorothy Bryan, "Marianne Strengell's Approach to Design," *Handweaver and Craftsman*, fall 1960, 29.

11. Sailors Papers, Cranbrook Archives, Cranbrook Academy of Art, Bloomfield Hills, MI.

12. Student records, Cranbrook Archives, Cranbrook Academy of Art, Bloom-field Hills, MI.

13. Gerhardt Knodel, interview by Loretta Oliver, June 24, 1998, transcript, MLH History Project Collection, MSU Museum.

14. Gerhardt Knodel, interview by authors, March 25, 2003, transcript, MLH History Project Collection, MSU Museum.

15. Knodel, interview by authors.

16. Knodel, letter to Marion Marzolf, January 26, 2005.

17. Jane Lackey, interview by Marion Marzolf, September 29, 2004, transcript, MLH History Project Collection, MSU Museum.

18. Dennis Barrie and Susan F. Rossen, "The School, 1926–1976," in Susan F. Rossen ed., *Arts and Crafts in Detroit*, 213–26.

19. Susan Aaron-Taylor, interview by Marion Marzolf, March 2, 2004.

20. Mollie Fletcher, interview by Marion Marzolf, October 1, 2004.

Chapter 5

1. *Shuttle-Craft Guild Bulletin*, September 1924, 1.

2. Hartland Area Historical Society, *Hartland*, 125.

3. A nineteen-minute video entitled *Wool Challenge* by Western Michigan University documents the sheep-to-shawl process. It is available through The Yarnbarn in Lawrence, Kansas.

4. Kay Boydston, "Successful Experiment: Michigan Group Explores Natural Dyes," *Handweaver and Craftsman*, winter 1963, 11, 40–41.

5. Niles Handweavers Guild Records, MLH History Project Collection, MSU Museum; Becky Voelker, "Giving Happens Year-Round at Library," *Daily Star* (Niles, MI), December 23, 1977, 6–7.

6. "To the Editor," SS&D, winter 1969, 8.

7. "Dorothea B. Buell, 1898–1972," 2, Buellwood Weavers Guild Records, MLH History Project Collection, MSU Museum.

8. Schedule of programs and activities, Michigan League of Handweavers Mary M. Atwater Memorial Conference, Waldenwoods, Hartland, MI, July 24–26, 1959, MLH History Project Collection, MSU Museum.

9. Records of the AuSable Manistee Weavers Guild, the Genesee Valley Fiber Guild, and the Eastside Handweavers Guild, MLH History Project Collection, MSU Museum.

10. Frances Hatch and Rosalind "Roz" Berlin, telephone interviews by Marie Gile, April 22, 2005.

11. Jo Graham, "Recollections of a Weaver: Jo Graham," *Fiber Connection* 22, no. 2 (winter 1983): 3–5.

12. Karol Blackaby, "Upswing in Fiber Arts: Guild for Spinners and Weavers Is Flourishing," *Chronicle* (Muskegon, MI), May 23, 1975, Women's section, 7–8.

13. Heidi Huntley, conversation with Marie Gile, January 14, 2002.

14. Kathleen Longcore, "Computers Loom Large in Weaving," *Grand Rapids Press*, July 22, 1984, B5.

15. Kalamazoo Valley Weavers' Guild History, Weavers Guild of Kalamazoo Records, MLH History Project Collection, MSU Museum.

16. Kalamazoo Valley Weavers' Guild History.

17. Mary Marlett, "Home Weaving 'Fascinating Craft' Say Members of Weaver's Guild," *Kalamazoo Gazette*, undated (ca. 1950s); Verne Berry, "Weaver Hobbyist

Spending Retirement Whittling Away," *Kalamazoo Gazette*, February 22, 1970, 30—both in MLH History Project Collection, MSU Museum.

18. Faye Sketchley, Fred Wessels' daughter-in-law, telephone interview by Marie Gile, March 5, 2003.

19. Alice Henwood, interview by Faye Wingate, June 1, 1998, transcript, MLH History Project Collection, MSU Museum.

20. Helen Coats, interview by Lestra Hazel, May 20, 1998, transcript, MLH History Project Collection, MSU Museum.

21. Sharon Ford, interview by Midge Lewis, July 16, 1998, transcript, MLH History Project Collection, MSU Museum.

22. Karen Kunze, interview by Midge Lewis, February 11, 1999, transcript, MLH History Project Collection, MSU Museum.

23. Elizabeth Clark, interview by Lestra Hazel, February 17, 1999, transcript, MLH History Project Collection, MSU Museum.

24. Brenda Mergen, interview by Faye Wingate, August 31, 1998, transcript, MLH History Project Collection, MSU Museum.

25. Esther James, "Remarks for December 8, 1997 Meeting," Weavers Guild of Kalamazoo Records, MLH History Project Collection, MSU Museum.

26. Bernice Sizemore, interview by Marie Gile, September 25, 2002, MLH History Project Collection, MSU Museum.

27. Bernice Sizemore, "The Founding of the Midland, Michigan FiberArts Guild," April 8, 2002, Midland FiberArts Guild Records, MLH History Project Collection, MSU Museum. Bernice Sizemore has been very generous in providing the authors with information about weaving in Michigan, particularly during the 1970s, including her research paper "The Organization and Current Implementation of Adult Weaving Programs in Selected Art Centers and Art Museums in Lower Michigan" (July 1978); a list of thirty-one weaving supply sources in Michigan in 1978; and brochures for fiber-art exhibits. These resources are now in the MLH History Project Collection, MSU Museum.

28. North Oakland Handweavers Guild Records, MLH History Project Collection, MSU Museum.

29. FinnWeavers Fiber Guild Records, MLH History Project Collection, MSU Museum.

30. Kay Holman, interview by Marie Gile, October 27, 2002; A. M. Kelley, "Weaver Melds Friendship with Joy," *Mining Journal* (Marquette, MI), October 30, 2002, 1.

31. Records of the Loomcrafters Guild, the Michigan Weavers Guild, and the Toledo Area Weavers Guild, MLH History Project Collection, MSU Museum.

32. Town and Country Weavers Records, MLH History Project Collection, MSU Museum.

33. "Dorothea M. Hulse Workshop, Detroit, Michigan, April 22–26, 1956," Jeanne Kish Collection, MLH History Project Collection, MSU Museum.

34. Carol Isleib, telephone interview by Marie Gile, April 7 and 8, 2005.

35. Records of the Michigan Handspinners Guild and the Delta Weavers Guild, MLH History Project Collection, MSU Museum.

36. Nancy Burkhalter, e-mail message to Marion Marzolf, February 20, 2005.

37. Marcia McDonald, telephone interview by Marion Marzolf, January 13, 2005.

38. Janet Jones Diones, interview by Marion Marzolf, January 12, 2005.

39. Mill Race Weavers Guild records, MLH History Project Collection, MSU Museum.

40. Hartland Area Historical Society, Hartland, 120.

41. Mill Race Weavers Guild Records, MLH History Project Collection, MSU Museum.

42. Quoted in Reiter, *Weaving a Life*, 148.

43. Greater Lansing Weavers Guild Records, MLH History Project Collection, MSU Museum; *Handweaver and Craftsman*, spring 1957, 28, 48.

44. Ann Arbor Fiberarts Guild Records, MLH History Project Collection, MSU Museum.

45. Katherine Lowrie, "Fiberarts Guild Is a Richly Textured Group," *Ann Arbor News*, November 1, 2003, Community Life, 3.

46. *Fiber Connection* 21, no. 2 (winter 1982): 4.

47. North Oakland Handweavers Guild Records, MLH History Project Collection, MSU Museum.

48. Rowland and Chinami Ricketts, program for the Ann Arbor Fiberarts Guild, January 11, 2005; information from the Web site http://www.rickettsindigo.com.

49. Jean Brudzinski, interview by Loretta Oliver, May 9, 1998.

Chapter 6

1. "Setting Up and Conducting First Adult Floor Loom Weaving Classes of Five Years or More Existence in Selected Lower Michigan Art Centers," Bernice Sizemore Papers, MLH History Project Collection, MSU Museum. This was a questionnaire for research by Bernice Sizemore, completed in the summer of 1978 by Helen Gleason, supervisor of University of Michigan Programs for Western Michigan (University of Michigan Extension Program) during the time weaving was taught at the Grand Rapids Art Gallery.

2. Betty Hagberg, interview by Kris Krumanaker, July 3, 1998, transcript, MLH History Project Collection, MSU Museum.

3. Jeffrey Kaczmarczyk, "Art Museum's Growth Surge, Changes Look Fine to Former Director McBride," *Grand Rapids Press*, January 13, 2002, B3; exhibition catalog published in conjunction with the exhibit *The Magic of Fibers*, 1970, Grand Rapids, MI, Walter McBride file, MLH History Project Collection, MSU Museum.

4. "Robert D. Sailors: Designer-Weaver for Architects, Interior Designers, and Decorators," *Handweaver and Craftsman*, fall 1965, 6–9.

5. Jochen Ditterich, interview by Marie Gile, April 8, 2002, transcript, MLH History Project Collection, MSU Museum.

6. Esther James, interview by Lestra Hazel, May 7, 1998, transcript, MLH History Project Collection, MSU Museum.

7. Helen Coats, interview by Lestra Hazel, May 20, 1998, transcript, MLH History Project Collection, MSU Museum.

8. Ditterich, interview.

9. "Double-Service Shop Sells Products of Hobbyists, Handicapped," *Grand Rapids Press*, May 14, 1956, MLH History Project Collection, MSU Museum.

10. Newspaper clippings, October 29, 1992, and September 24, 1961, McGarr Family History Papers, "Looms" File, MLH History Project Collection, MSU Museum.

11. Jane Patrick, "Cranbrook Loom," *Handwoven*, September/October 2002, 67–69.

12. Esther James, "Remarks for December 8, 1997 Meeting," Weavers Guild of Kalamazoo Records, MLH History Project Collection, MSU Museum.

13. Bernice Sizemore, "The Organization and Current Implementation of Adult

Weaving Programs in Selected Art Centers and Art Museums in Lower Michigan," July 1978, MLH History Project Collection, MSU Museum.

14. Bernice Sizemore, interview by Marie Gile, September 25, 2002, MLH History Project Collection, MSU Museum; e-mail correspondence with Marie Gile, August 28, 2005.

15. "Program of Weaving Group Told," *Midland Daily News*, March 21, 1973.

16. Lillian Holm was very active during these years, teaching not only at the Kingswood School at Cranbrook but at the Cranbrook Academy of Art after 1934 and at Flint Institute of Arts. In 1936, she headed the Works Progress Administration's Federal Art Project in the Upper Peninsula, as referenced by Mark Coir, director of Cranbrook Archives, in "Lillian Holm: Creator of an Artistic Legacy," *Tradition*, n.d., 24–25, Cranbrook Archives, Cranbrook Academy of Art, Bloomfield Hills, MI.

17. Research by Bernice Sizemore, specifically a questionnaire completed by Jennie Warren for Flint Institute of Arts weaving program, 1977–78, Bernice Sizemore Papers, MLH History Project Collection, MSU Museum.

18. Alice Foster, telephone interview by Marie Gile, January 7, 2005.

19. "Eleen Auvil: Versatile Designer Weaver," *Handweaver and Craftsman*, winter 1969, 11, 45.

20. Barbara Wittenberg, interview by Nancy Peck, August 17, 1998, transcript, MLH History Project Collection, MSU Museum.

21. Mary Lou Koval, telephone interview by Marie Gile, February 4, 2005. Koval recalled that during a workshop on bog jackets given by Wittenberg to the Greater Lansing Weavers Guild, Wittenberg read letters from her daughter who was in Africa in the Peace Corps at the time. While workshop participants wove their garments, Wittenberg shared letters and stories about life in Africa that related customs and communicated the culture of the weavers of kente cloth.

22. Barbara Wittenberg, interview by Nancy Peck, August 17, 1998.

23. Robert Kidd, telephone interview by Marion Marzolf, January 5, 2005.

24. Sue Walton, e-mail correspondence with Marion Marzolf, January 24, 2005.

25. "Weavers, Weaving Guilds, and Weaving Shops: The Dearborn Handweaving Studio," *Warp and Weft* 13, no. 10 (December 1960): 3.

26. Libby Crawford, interview by Lestra Hazel, October 2, 1998.

27. Nancy Peck, interview by Karen Yackell, February 22, 1999, transcript, MLH History Project Collection, MSU Museum.

28. Nancy Peck, e-mail message to Marion Marzolf, January 5, 2005.

29. Nancy Peck, e-mail message to Marion Marzolf, January 15, 2005.

30. Nancy Peck, interview by Karen Yackell and Loretta Oliver, February 22, 1999, transcripts, MLH History Project Collection, MSU Museum.

31. "Craftsmen: Artist-Craftsmen Exhibition in Michigan," *Handweaver and Craftsman*, summer 1951, 25–26.

32. Shirley Woodson-Reid, interview by Marion Marzolf, January 13, 2005.

33. "Prominent Weaver Joyce Jones Dies," *Ann Arbor News*, February 3, 1980, A3.

34. The Michigan yarn retailers listed for 1972 are Mariposa Handweavers (Traverse City), The Weaver Bird (Muskegon), The Weaver's Shop and Yarn Company (Rockford), The Yarn Merchant (Kalamazoo), Fiberworks (Flint), Rapunzel's (Frankenmuth), Beyond the Fringe (Rochester), The Golden Heddle (Royal Oak), McBean's Yarn and Weavers (at Singers) (Alma), Traditional Handicrafts (Northville), Wool Findings, Inc. (Free Soil), The Weaving Shop (Baldwin), Nif-T Corner (Coldwater), Wild Weft Yarns (Ann Arbor), and Davidson's Old Mill Yarns (Eaton Rapids).

35. Patty Beyer, president of Yarnwinders Fiber Guild in Marquette, e-mail correspondence with Marie Gile, April 10, 2005.

Chapter 7

1. Eunice Anders, interview by Nancy Peck, May 5, 1998, MLH History Project Collection, MSU Museum.

2. Patti Aikin, "Waldenwoods: Weaving in Hartland," *Fiber Connection* 21, no. 4 (summer 1982): 6–8.

3. Alice Griswold, interview by Marie Gile, January 21, 2005.

4. A. M. Kelley, "Weaver Melds Friendship with Joy," *Mining Journal* (Marquette, MI), October 30, 2002, 1.

5. Loraine Kessenich, "Weaving an Artificial Valve for the Human Heart," MLH Newsletter, fall 1979.

6. Waagen, "American Handweaving" (PhD diss.), 52.

7. Paul J. Smith, ed., *Objects for Use: Handmade by Design* (New York: Harry N. Abrams and American Craft Museum, 2001), 16.

8. Irene Waller, *Textile Sculptures* (London: Studio Vista, 1977), 10.

9. Anni Albers, "Handweaving Today," *Weaver* 6, no. 1 (January/February 1941): 3–9.

10. Mary Atwater, "It's Lovely—but Is It Art?" *Weaver* 6, no. 3 (July/August 1941): 13–14, 26.

11. Quoted in Waagen, "American Handweaving" (PhD diss.), 51–56, 134–35.

12. "Fabrics from the Looms of Karl Laurell," *Handweaver and Craftsman*, fall 1951, 9–10, 52.

13. "Plymouth Colony Farms," *Handweaver and Craftsman*, spring 1950.

14. "Fabrics from the Looms of Karl Laurell," 52.

15. Paul J. Smith, "Reflections: 20th Century Fiber History in America," *Friends of Fiber Art International News*, no. 32, April 2002, 1–4.

16. Lili Blumenau, *The Art and Craft of Hand Weaving* (New York: Crown Publishers, 1955).

17. Quoted in Alice K. Waagen, "American Handweaving: The Postwar Years," *Handwoven*, May/June 1990, 50.

18. Jack Lenor Larsen, "The Weaver as Artist," *Craft Horizons*, November/December 1955, 33.

19. Although there is not much information about Hallco Hand Weavers, one historic home in Hudson has a large variety of the company's work. A few sources were located at the Hudson Public Library. A tribute written for Louise Cornes in 1954, shortly after her death, states: "the last 16 years of her life were spent in Hudson living with her cousin, Florence Hall. During the first part of this period, she worked as a bookkeeper . . . and when no longer physically able to leave her home, she continued this type of work at the house . . . She also took up weaving and in this field her work was of such excellence that she was chosen by the State Rehabilitation Association to demonstrate it to other workers. For this purpose she attended a two-day state meeting where her work was pronounced outstanding for the originality of design and the excellence of craftsmanship. Her work also received honorable mention by the Toledo Museum of Art at one of its annual art exhibits." An article by Catherine Stucky, "Hudson Salutes Miss Florence Hall" (*Hudson Post Gazette*, February 13, 1969), states that Florence Hall was an English teacher at Hudson High School and, after her retirement, a "long time beloved Librarian" in Hudson.

20. *Woven by the Griswolds, East Lansing, Michigan* (Midland, MI: Midland Art Council, Midland Center for the Arts, 1989), 1. This exhibition catalog was published in conjunction with an exhibition showing September 9–October 9, 1989, at the Midland Center for the Arts.

21. Alice Griswold, interview by Marie Gile, January 21, 2005. The Griswolds purchased their first power loom through the help of Dexter Blake, who supervised the weaving room at Jackson Prison in Jackson, Michigan. Blake had a power loom that he had purchased from Horner Woolen Mill in Eaton Rapids and that he operated in his garage. He did custom weaving for architects on the West Coast. With Blake's help, the Griswolds were able to purchase a power loom that had originally been used at a mill in Pittsburgh, Pennsylvania. Blake also helped them learn to operate the power loom. At the time, Jackson Prison wove articles for various state institutions. Weaving has also been taught as a creative activity in prisons. In 1987, art graduate student Ann Plevin wrote an article entitled "Teaching at a Men's Prison" (*Fiberarts*, January/February 1987, 36–37), in which she describes teaching weaving to inmates at Michigan's Huron Valley Men's Facility "to cultivate creative expression in an artistically arid environment."

22. Alice Griswold, interview by Marie Gile, April 11, 2005.

23. *Woven by the Griswolds*, 2.

24. Alice Griswold, *Weaving Solutions* (Milan, MI: A and G Publications, 2000), vii.

25. Friends of the Fleece Records, MLH History Project Collection, MSU Museum.

26. Dottie Goodwin, interview by Lestra Hazel, January 27, 1999, transcript, MLH History Project Collection, MSU Museum.

27. Elizabeth Colburn, interview by Marie Gile, September 19, 2002, transcript, MLH History Project Collection, MSU Museum.

28. "Scientific Research Suggests Ideas for Fabric Designs," *Handweaver and Craftsman*, summer 1964, 5–6, 41.

29. April Kingsley, "Unraveling the Weave," *Fiberarts*, March/April 1995, 45–51.

30. Mildred Constantine and Jack Lenor Larsen, *Beyond Craft: The Art Fabric* (New York: Van Nostrand Reinhold, 1973).

31. Gerhardt Knodel, interview by authors, March 25, 2003, transcript, MLH History Project Collection, MSU Museum.

32. Donna Olendorf, "Gerhardt Knodel," *Fiberarts*, November/December 1978, 44–47. Knodel's "Free Fall" was later removed in a major renovation of the Renaissance Center.

33. Jochen Ditterich, interview by Marie Gile, April 8, 2002, transcript, MLH History Project Collection, MSU Museum.

34. Rosalind "Roz" Berlin, "Artist's Statement 1999," MLH History Project Collection, MSU Museum.

35. "Forest Takes Root," *Saginaw News*, March 6, 2004, Weekend Arts, 1.

36. Kati Reeder Meek, *Reflections from a Flaxen Past: For Love of Lithuanian Weaving* (Alpena, MI: Penannular Press International, 2000).

37. Lynn Baldwin, "Clothing as Canvas: The Artistry of Chris Triola," *A2 Lifestyle Magazine* 4, no. 4 (2003): 12–13; information from the Web site http://www.christriola.com.

38. Joanne Mattera, "Making a Place for Technology in the Fiber Arts," *Fiberarts*, March/April 1982, 6.

39. Margaret Windeknecht, e-mail correspondence with Marie Gile, March 27, 2003.

40. Margaret Windeknecht and Thomas Windeknecht, "Color-and-Weave on a Dark-Light Sequence," *SS&D*, fall 1981, 24–27; Marjorie O'Shaugnessy, review of

Color-and-Weave, by Margaret Windeknecht and Thomas Windeknecht, SS&D, fall 1981, 62–63; Anne A. D'Angelo and Margaret M. Windeknecht, "Batik Plus Handweaving," SS&D, summer 1973, cover, 4, 57–58; Bill Laitner, "Reweaving a Life: 'Stroke Victor' Is Model for Others," *Detroit Free Press,* May 21, 1986, B1, 4; Alexis Yiorgos Xenakis, "A Time to Revitalize," *Prairie Wool Companion* 4, no. 1, issue 11 (1985), 10–13; Windeknecht, e-mail correspondence with Marie Gile.

41. Verda Elliott, interview by Karen Yackell, June 8, 1998, transcript, MLH History Project Collection, MSU Museum.

42. Verda Elliott, introduction to her class notes for drafting with a computer, Michigan League of Handweavers Biennial Conference "Color Connections," June 1990, 1.

43. "One Hundred Years of American Craft," *AmericanStyle,* spring 2000, 31–38; information from the Web site http://www.sofaexpo.com.

44. Marion Marzolf, "A Felting Journey: Inspiring Teachers and Experimentation Have Guided Loretta Oliver's Explorations of a Medium," *Fiberarts,* March/April 2004, 36–38.

Chapter 8

1. Verna Suit, "The Guild Phenomenon: A History Lesson," SS&D, spring 1957, 52–55.

2. Panel discussion, Detroit Handweavers Tenth Anniversary Program, International Institute, Detroit, MI, April 11, 1958, MLH History Project Collection, MSU Museum.

3. "Minutes of First Group Meeting of a Proposed Michigan State Organization of Handweavers," November 3, 1958, MLH History Project Collection, MSU Museum.

4. "Minutes of Organization Committee, State of Michigan Association of Handweavers," December 1, 1958, MLH History Project Collection, MSU Museum.

5. "Minutes of Organization Committee, Michigan League of Handweavers," February 2, 1959, MLH History Project Collection, MSU Museum.

6. "Weavers Shoptalk," *Handweaver and Craftsman,* winter 1960, 56.

7. Helen Hill, "Report of the President of MLH," July 22, 1960, MLH Historic Records, Old Mill Yarns, Eaton Rapids, Michigan.

8. "Michigan League of Handweavers," *Handweaver and Craftsman,* fall 1965, 4; brochure of the annual conference of the Michigan League of Handweavers, Grand Rapids, Michigan, June 18–20, 1965, MLH History Project Collection, MSU Museum.

9. JoAnn Bachelder, interview by Marie Gile, August 9, 2004, transcript, MLH History Project Collection, MSU Museum.

10. Michigan League of Handweavers membership flyer, 2002–4, and minutes of a meeting of the Michigan League of Handweavers, March 13, 2004, MLH History Project Collection, MSU Museum.

11. Susie Henzie, "The First Fifteen Years, " SS&D, winter 1984, 44, and "A Brief Report," SS&D, fall 1977, 4–6.

12. "In the Beginning" and "Tabby," SS&D, winter 1969, 1, 3.

13. Convention program, SS&D, spring 1972, 10.

14. Else Regensteiner, "Tradition, Innovation—and Identity," SS&D, spring 1970, 3.

15. Mary Sayler, interview by Lestra Hazel, June 11, 1998, transcript, MLH History Project Collection, MSU Museum.

16. Gerhardt Knodel, interview by Loretta Oliver, June 24, 1998, transcript, MLH History Project Collection, MSU Museum.

17. Convergence '72 program, SS&D, spring 1972, 22–23.

18. Harriet Tidball, *Contemporary Costume: Strictly Handwoven*, Shuttle Craft Monograph Twenty-four (Lansing, MI: Shuttle Craft Guild, 1968). Weavers Tonya Rhodes, teaching at Western Michigan University in Kalamazoo, and Nell Scott of Toppenish, Washington, were also featured as clothing designers in this monograph.

19. Rosalind Berlin, telephone conversation with Marie Gile, December 20, 2004.

20. Barbara Wittenberg, *Alternatives to a Fig Leaf* (Southfield, MI: Barbara Wittenberg, 1972).

21. Sandra Lummen, telephone conversation with Marion Marzolf, August 14, 2004; Marj Mink, telephone conversation with Marion Marzolf, February 1, 2004.

Chapter 9

1. Kerstin Sjöqvist, *Trasuäv: Rag Weavings* (Stockholm: Nordiska Museet, 1967), 2.

2. Jane Fredlund, *Rag Rug Weaves: Patterns from Sweden* (Stockholm: LTs Forlag, 1986), 8.

3. Keijo Virtanen, *The Finns in the United States: The Project on Finnish Immigration of the Michigan Historical Collections*, Michigan Historical Collections Bulletin 26 (Ann Arbor: University of Michigan, 1975), 3.

4. The material for this chapter comes primarily from the lecture "Rags, Rugs, and Weavers" presented at the Michigan State University Museum in East Lansing on November 20, 2004. It is rewritten and used with the permission of the researchers. Dr. Lockwood is preparing the study for scholarly publication. Other sources used are noted.

5. Janet Meany and Paula Pfaff, *Rag Rug Handbook* (Loveland, CO: Interweave Press, 1996), 88–89.

Chapter 10

1. There may be other colleges that briefly offered weaving, but information is scant. For example, a ceramics professor at Northern Michigan University in Marquette in the 1990s offered fiber classes for a few years, but the classes stopped when he retired. The Art Institute of Chicago offered weaving and fiber classes during some of its summer programs at Oxbow, near Saugatuck.

2. "Industrial Ed Vital since 1901," *Ypsilanti Press*, April 19, 1966; clipping, Eastern Michigan University Bruce T. Halle Library and Archives, Ypsilanti, MI.

3. *Michigan State Normal College Bulletin*, 1940–76 (Ypsilanti, MI: Michigan State Normal College, 1940–76).

4. Elizabeth Francis-Connolly, telephone interview by Marion Marzolf, November 16, 2004.

5. "Dorothy Lamming to Retire after 29 Years at EMU," *Ann Arbor News*, June 26, 1971, Eastern Michigan University Bruce T. Halle Library and Archives, Ypsilanti, MI.

6. Pat Williams, interview by Marion Marzolf, August 30, 2004, transcript, MLH History Project Collection, MSU Museum.

7. Julie Becker, telephone interview by Marion Marzolf, February 15, 2005.

8. Cathryn Amidei, e-mail message to Marion Marzolf, February 15, 2005.

9. Subhas Ghosh, telephone interview by Marion Marzolf, February 15, 2005.

10. *Michigan State Agricultural College Catalogue* (East Lansing, MI: Michigan State Agricultural College, 1896), 26, 94–95.

11. Sally Helvenston, interview by authors, October 4, 2004, transcript, MLH History Project Collection, MSU Museum.

12. *Michigan State Agricultural College Catalog*, 1920–60.

13. "Academic Programs for 1972/73," in *Michigan State University Catalog*, 1972 (East Lansing, MI: Michigan State University, 1972).

14. "Academic Programs for 1972/73," 161.

15. Martha Brownscombe, interview by authors, January 15, 2005, transcript, MLH History Project Collection, MSU Museum.

16. Grace "Ronny" Martin, letter to Martha Brownscombe, February 4, 2005.

17. Brownscombe, interview.

18. Helvenston, e-mail message to Marion Marzolf, January 25, 2005.

19. Richard Cooper, e-mail interview by Marion Marzolf, January 19, 2005. Some Michigan state prisons have taught weaving in their art opportunity programs, as described by Ann Plevin in "Teaching at a Men's Prison," *Fiberarts*, January/February 1987, 36–37.

20. Undated clipping, Western Michigan University Libraries, Kalamazoo, MI; *Western Michigan University Bulletin*, 1965, 70, 110.

21. Eve Reid, telephone interview by Marion Marzolf, December 30, 2004.

22. "Eleen Auvil: Versatile Designer Weaver," *Handweaver and Craftsman*, winter 1969.

23. Urban Jupena, telephone interview by Marion Marzolf, October 21, 2004, transcript, MLH History Project Collection, MSU Museum.

24. Jupena, telephone interview.

25. *Central Michigan University Bulletin*, 1944–84, Central Michigan University Libraries, Mount Pleasant, MI.

26. Bernice Sizemore, interview by Marie Gile, February 28, 2005.

27. Katherine Ux, "On Teaching Weaving," *Handweaver and Craftsman*, summer 1960, 48–49.

28. Sally Rose, interview by authors, August 16, 2004, transcript, MLH History Project Collection, MSU Museum.

29. Wendell Heers, telephone interview by Marion Marzolf, October 6, 2004.

30. Sherri Smith, interview by Marion Marzolf, August 2, 2004, transcript, MLH History Project Collection, MSU Museum.

31. Smith, interview.

32. Smith, interview.

33. Elizabeth Leifer, telephone interview by Marion Marzolf, October 17, 2004, and letter to Marion Marzolf, October 15, 2004.

34. Phyllis Fredendall, "Personal Histories of Members of the Buellwood Weavers Guild and Other Weavers from the Copper Country of Keweenaw Peninsula of Upper Michigan," January 2003, MLH History Project Collection, MSU Museum.

35. Phyllis Fredendall, e-mail message to Marion Marzolf, February 20, 2004.

36. Sister Jean Agnes Klemm, OP, telephone interview by Marion Marzolf, October 7, 2004.

37. Sandra Lummen, telephone interview by Marion Marzolf, August 14, 2004.

38. Albert Story, telephone interview by Marion Marzolf, November 16, 2004. Story is director of the University of Michigan Extension Program. The art museum's

archives are not accessible. Interviews from Lummen and Story and the museum's guide for docents were useful.

Chapter 11

1. Waller, *Textile Sculptures*, 13.
2. Rob Pulleyn, "Goodbye from Rob Pulleyn," *Fiberarts*, March/April 2004, 3–4.

Selected Bibliography

The authors conducted a broad range of interviews with weavers, teachers, guild officers, and students and made extensive use of oral histories and guild scrapbooks prepared for the Michigan League of Handweavers history project, for which Marie A. Gile served as principal researcher. The papers and transcripts gathered for the MLH history project are housed in a collection at the Michigan State University Museum in East Lansing, Michigan. The archives of the Michigan League of Handweavers are housed at Old Mill Yarns in Eaton Rapids, Michigan. Several local and specialized archives were also helpful. Newsletters, craft magazines, and clipping files were also consulted. All sources are documented in the notes. Listed here are selected works cited in the text and notes.

Alvic, Philis. *Weavers of the Southern Highlands.* Lexington: University Press of Kentucky, 2003.

Anderson, Clarita S. *Weaving a Legacy: The Don and Jean Stuck Coverlet Collection.* Columbus, OH: Columbus Museum of Art and Harry N. Abrams, 1995.

Atwater, Mary Meigs. *Byways in Hand-Weaving.* New York: Macmillan, 1954.

———. *The Shuttle-Craft Book of American Handweaving.* 1928. Reprint. New York: Macmillan, 1947.

Broudy, Eric. *The Book of Looms.* Hanover, NH: University Press of New England, 1979.

Brown, Katharine McGregor. "Michigan's Pioneer Coverlet Weaver: A Study of Abram William Van Doren's Seven Years of Coverlet Weaving in Avon Township, Michigan, 1844 to 1851." Master's thesis, Wayne State University, 1982.

Bryan, Ford R. *Beyond the Model T.* Detroit: Wayne State University Press, 1980.

Clark, Robert Judson, et al. *Design in America: The Cranbrook Vision, 1925–1950.* New York: Harry N. Abrams, 1983.

Constantine, Mildred, and Jack Lenor Larsen. *Beyond Craft: The Art Fabric.* New York: Van Nostrand Reinhold, 1973.

Crockett, Norman L. *The Woolen Industry of the Midwest.* Lexington: University Press of Kentucky, 1970.

Fredlund, Jane. *Rag Rug Weaves: Patterns from Sweden.* Stockholm: LTs Forlag, 1986.

Galbraith, D. James. *Hartland: Change in the Heart of America.* Hartland, MI: Galbraith-Scott Publications, ca. 1985.

Griswold, Alice. *Weaving Solutions.* Milan, MI: A and G Publications, 2000.

Harris, Jennifer, ed. *5000 Years of Textiles.* New York: Harry N. Abrams, 1993.

Hartland Area Historical Society. *Hartland: Weaving the Past with the Present*. Hartland, MI: Hartland Area Historical Society, 2004.

Lyford, Carrie A. *Ojibwa Crafts*. 1943. Reprint, Stevens Point, WI: R. Schneider, 1982.

Meany, Janet, and Paula Pfaff. *Rag Rug Handbook*. Loveland, CO: Interweave Press, 1996.

Meek, Kati Reeder. *Reflections from a Flaxen Past: For Love of Lithuanian Weaving*. Alpena, MI: Penannular Press International, 2000.

Michigan: A Guide to the Wolverine State. New York: Oxford University Press, 1941.

Penney, David W. *Native Arts of North America*. Trans. Peter Snowden. Paris: Editions Pierre Terrail, 1998.

Pennington, Dave. *A Pictorial Guide to American Spinning Wheels*. Sabbath Lake, ME: Shaker Press, 1975.

Reiter, Mary Jo. *Weaving a Life: The Story of Mary Meigs Atwater*. Loveland, CO: Interweave Press, 1992.

Rossen, Susan F., ed. *Arts and Crafts in Detroit, 1906–1976: The Movement, the Society, the School*. Detroit: Detroit Institute of Arts, 1976.

Sjöqvist, Kerstin. *Trasuäv: Rag Weavings*. Stockholm: Nordiska Museet, 1967.

Smith, Paul J., ed. *Objects for Use: Handmade by Design*. New York: Harry N. Abrams and American Craft Museum, 2001.

Squires, Clara, and Jean Kline. *Island City Pictorial History, 1835–1980*. Eaton Rapids, MI, Squires, 1980.

Tidball, Harriet. *Contemporary Costume: Strictly Handwoven*. Shuttle Craft Monograph Twenty-four. Lansing, MI: Shuttle Craft Guild, 1968.

———. *Contemporary Tapestry*. Shuttle Craft Monograph Twelve. Lansing, MI: Shuttle Craft Guild, 1964.

U.S. Tariff Commission. *The Wool Growing Industry*. Washington: U.S. Government Printing Office, 1921.

Virtanen, Keijo. *The Finns in the United States: The Project on Finnish Immigration of the Michigan Historical Collections*. Michigan Historical Collections Bulletin 26. Ann Arbor: University of Michigan, 1975.

Waagen, Alice K. "An Historical Survey and Analysis of American Handweaving." PhD diss., Pennsylvania State University, 1982.

Waller, Irene. *Textile Sculptures*. London: Studio Vista, 1977.

Wilson, Kax. *A History of Textiles*. Boulder, CO: Westview Press, 1979.

Wittenberg, Barbara. *Alternatives to a Fig Leaf*. Southfield, MI: Barbara Wittenberg, 1972.

Woodford, Frank B., and Albert Hyma. *Gabriel Richard, Frontier Ambassador*. Detroit: Wayne State University Press, 1958.